Enjoy your

TRUE POWER

Linda Larsen

TRUE POWER

Get It, Use It, Share it

Ten smart strategies to get what you want out of life

Linda Larsen

Brandywine Publishing

Manufactured in the United States of America
Library of Congress Catalog Card Number: 00-90077
ISBN: 0-9678084-0-5
Book design and production by Tabby House
Cover design: Osprey Design Systems

Publisher's Cataloging-in-Publication
(Provided by Quality Books, Inc.)

Larsen, Linda, 1948-
    True Power : get it, use it, share it : ten
strategies for gaining more power and contol in
your life, using it wisely and sharing it
unabashedly / Linda Larsen -- 1st edition
      p. cm.
    Includes biographical references and index
    LCCN: 00-90077
    ISBN: 0-9678084-0-5

    1. Control (Psychology) 2. Power (Philosophy)
I. Title.

BF611.L37 2000   158.1
                      QBI00-233

Brandywine Publishing
P. O. Box 15024
Sarasota, FL 34277

Contents

Dedication	*ix*
Acknowledgments	*xi*
Introduction	*xiii*
Strategy No. 1: Get Conscious	19
Strategy No. 2: Create a Rich, Vivid Vision	29
Strategy No. 3: Make Up Your Own Stories	39
Strategy No. 4: Trust the Unseen Forces	51
Strategy No. 5: Make Lots of Good Impressions	61
Strategy No. 6: Be a Solution Provider	71
Strategy No. 7: Build Strong Relationships	83
Strategy No. 8: Communicate Wisely	93
Strategy No. 9: Master Your Emotions	103
Strategy No. 10: Practice Lifelong Learning	115
Conclusion	125
Bibliography	131
Index	133
About the author	*143*

Dedication

I dedicate this book in memory of
my beautiful, talented mother, June,
and my loving, courageous father, Peter.

Acknowledgments

I am so blessed and fortunate to have a group of individuals who have loved, supported and encouraged me prior to and throughout the creation of this book. It is with the deepest appreciation that I acknowledge the following people:

Christopher Young for trusting his good instincts and supporting me in this venture; as always, David Owen Ritz for being my friend and for sharing his tremendous wisdom and insights with me; my family, Ginny, Jerry and Michael Scalzi, Rocky Lomeo, Karen Zendels, and Shivan Sarna for being my best unconditional love-givers; my faraway family, the LoPriores, Tartaglias and Vanacores and my fairy god-family, Janet and Stanley Kane. Also, thanks to my SkillPath family and my many friends and teachers at the Asolo Theater and Conservatory (Brant, Manuel, Neal and Jimmy) and my much-treasured Golden Apple Turoffs.

My never-ending gratitude also goes to Bruce Rodgers for sharing his creativity and his outstanding ideas; my amazing, beloved Ruby Allen who will always be my most cherished friend and advisor. To Michael Dobson, for his outstanding literary advice and my fabulous publicists, Pam and Rick Lontos.

Then there are the great "buds" who make all things possible through their love, support and cheerleading efforts: Kathy Mendel, Rick DeFuria, Garry Jackson, Mary Lee Richey, Janice Midkiff, Sandy Watson, Jenai, Jaime

Wallace, Linda Kauffmann, Terry McKee, Lynette Mancuso, Donna Dougherty, Phil and Shirley LaScelle, Jorge and Alina Fernandez, Richard and Jill London, Laurent Nahon and Madeline Dougherty.

I will always be indebted to Alice and Jared Massanari and Emil Codol, my pillars of strength who were always there when I needed them, and Dale Townsend who told me the truth even when I didn't want to hear it—what a gift! Thank you, Anthony Robbins for teaching me how to get into action.

And finally, I extend my deepest, heartfelt appreciation to my son, Miles, for being one of my greatest teachers and my richest source of joy; and to my husband, John Scalzi, for making me laugh, for being my computer wizard, massage master, chef extraordinaire and the absolute love of my life.

Introduction

Power, n. *(Mod. Fr.* pouvoir*) to be able; ability to act; capability of producing an effect; strength, force, or energy manifested in action.*—The New Webster Encyclopedic Dictionary

He slowly lifts his gun and aims it directly between my eyes. He methodically cocks the hammer, closes one eye, as if for greater accuracy, and with a thin voice asks, "Are you ready to die?"

I am frozen. As I stare down the barrel of his .357 Magnum, I am acutely aware of the split. There are two of me—two distinct people in my head, each jockeying for first position, for control over the ultimate outcome. The Survivor is calculating escape strategies at breakneck speed, analyzing every minute detail with superior precision. She has one intention—to get me out of this nightmare alive.

As odd as it seems, she has one obstacle even greater than the escaped convict with nothing to lose on the other end of the gun. She has to deal with the other me, the Panic Stricken One, the one running around in circles, arms flailing wildly, screaming, crying, groveling for mercy. This one is completely out of control. The insane situation has total power over her and her sensibilities. The Survivor, on the other hand, is wielding her power over the situation. In the face of this madman she has an enormous advantage. Her power is extremely channeled and focused with pinpoint accuracy on its target. She knows exactly what to do.

After a carefully calculated pause, the Survivor speaks, slowly and deliberately, "If you're going to kill me, I guess there's not much I can do to stop you."

I watch the words float out into space and hang in the air. The Panic Stricken One is screaming inside my head, "What did you say *that* for, you idiot? Quick! Take it back! Take it back!"

The man continues to point his gun at me. Time is now suspended with a surreal echo in what seems like forever. Finally, he slowly lowers the gun. His eyes narrow slightly as his head cocks imperceptibly to the right.

"Why aren't you down on the floor begging and pleading for your life?" he asks.

The Survivor quickly scans her computer-brain for the correct response. Ah, there it is. She takes a purposeful breath, looks him directly in the eye and with the exact right mix of respect and confidence, she responds, "Because you are in control of this situation. If you want to kill me, you can. There's nothing I can do. You are in control. You have the power."

And for the first time since this horror began three hours earlier, the man looks confused.

In this moment I get it. *I* have the power. *I* am in control. *I am* the Survivor. In my mind I square off with the Panic Stricken One and grab her by the shoulders. I tell her to relax, leave it to me, and trust. I assure her that I know what to do and I will get us out alive. And that is exactly what I do.

Now, looking back on that dramatic event, I have a wider perspective. I see that the entire experience was a tremendous life lesson about power. In the days and weeks that followed I not only began the process of dealing with the obvious trauma to my system, but I also began to see the experience as a metaphor for how to gain control and power in my life—no matter what the circumstances. I saw that there were distinct parallels to be drawn between that event, and other challenging situations in my life.

What I experienced of power as I was growing up was anything but positive. I was raised in a home with an alcoholic mother and a substantial amount of physical and mental abuse. By the age of twenty I was married and divorced with a baby. I also began having severe, debilitating panic attacks around that time. In fact, the morning I was kidnapped, Pearl Harbor Day, 1969, I had woken up and within minutes slipped into that familiar place of terror. I seriously thought of suicide. I was filled with a depressive sense of dread—that if I had to live my life like this—hanging on to my sanity by a flimsy string, I simply could not do it. I wanted out. But in spite of my emotions, I forced myself to go to work.

Isn't it extremely ironic that four hours later an escaped convict would ask me if I was ready to die and offer me a one way ticket out?

What I later began to realize is that my life up until that time had been a theme song for living in a state of powerlessness and despair. Certainly anyone who has lived with an alcoholic parent knows well the sense of helplessness which permeates his or her life. And the choices I continually made after I left home were ones subconsciously designed to keep me in that familiar state.

I believe (and this is merely an interpretation on my part) that my being kidnapped and held hostage for five hours was a huge gift to me. It was as if it was God's way of saying, "OK, you think you want to die. I happen to know that you have amazing, wonderful things to accomplish in this life. I know that your life has the potential to be absolutely rich with joy and abundance and positive power. But if you can't see that right now, I guess I have to resort to putting you in a situation where you will see it."

I'm not sure I could have gotten it any other way.

So, after "liberation day" I became a serious student. I began to explore this elusive thing called Power. I wanted to know how I could consciously access it and use it in all domains of my life. I wanted to know, more specifically, how I could use it *positively* for my advantage and for the advantage of others.

What I learned was that there are ways that we can gain control *in* our lives—*over* our lives—in order to consciously create the outcomes we desire. Notice I didn't say anything about having power over *other* people. The odd paradox is that the more control and power we exert within ourselves, the stronger we become in the eyes of other people, which gives us more influence with them.

My research and study also led me to the belief that there are ten very specific strategies we can use to help us get more power in our lives—strategies that we can apply to help us get our desired results in life. And what I also realized was that the first task was to get extremely clear about exactly what these "desired results" were. I understood that I could never attain anything in my life that I couldn't define or create a mental equivalent of.

As you read this book, I ask you to also get very clear on exactly what having more power and control in your life will do for you. What will it look like—how will it manifest in your life—when you are in a position of power? How will you know when you have it? What will it feel like?

Also, be aware that your initial thoughts may change as you entertain some of the ideas in this book. Remember, I am speaking of what I call *true power*. It's the kind of power Ralph Ellison must have been speaking of when he said, "Power doesn't have to show off. Power is confident, self-assuring, self-starting and self-stopping, self-warming and self-justifying. When you have it, you know it."

There is also an *illusion* of power, which is neither good nor bad, but rather a tool for you to use for a positive purpose. This is the kind of power referred to by Saul Alinsky when he said, "Power is not only what you have but what the enemy thinks you have." You will discover that using the illusion of power could actually help create the reality of it in your life.

Regardless of the type of power that you are utilizing, let's look at the types of outcome these strategies are designed to give you. These outcomes apply both personally and professionally.

- A feeling of competence to handle life's challenges
- A sense of being in control of your emotions
- Respect from your peers and associates
- More credibility
- Greater confidence
- The ability to trust yourself and your abilities
- The ability to choose what is right for you based on what *you* decide.
- Stronger relationships with others
- Peace of mind
- Greater rapport building skills
- The ability to create the material wealth and abundance that you desire—and deserve
- Less stress
- Better health, mentally and physically
- Heightened awareness
- Better communication skills
- The ability to ask for what you need
- More fun!

These are some of the outcomes this book is designed to help you achieve. There are more, which you will discover as you begin to apply the ten strategies for success.

Each chapter covers one of the strategies. You will be best served if, upon concluding one of the chapters, you will immediately put the idea into practice in your life. Since this may be a new or different concept, it may at first seem awkward. I will tell you now that people who are not committed to creating a different reality in their lives will try a new strategy once, hate the feeling of discomfort with the unfamiliar, and give up. They will proclaim, "Oh, I tried. Those ideas don't work."

This almost seems as ludicrous to me as hearing a one-year-old toddler exclaim after trying to walk the first time, "Oh, to heck with this. This walking thing doesn't work. I'll just be a crawler for the rest of my life." Of course not. That child recognized that this thing called "walking" was a strategy that would help her get what she wanted in life and she stuck with it until she succeeded.

I encourage you to do the same thing. If you do, if you commit one hundred percent to the ideas and techniques contained in this book, and if you take consistent daily action toward your goal, you will be successful. You will have the kind of life that you deserve. You will live with True Power.

Strategy No. 1

Get Conscious

If you choose unconsciously, you evolve unconsciously. If you choose consciously, you evolve consciously.—Gary Zukav

Have you ever driven somewhere, and when you arrived it suddenly occurred to you that you had no memory of the actual drive? You don't remember stopping at signals, turning, other vehicles, or any details of the trip. It's simultaneously funny and a little frightening. How did you get there safely? The answer can be found in the following riddle:

I am your constant companion.

I am your greatest helper or your heaviest burden.

I will push you onward or drag you down to failure.

I am completely at your command.

Half the things you do you might just as well turn over to me and I will be able to do them quickly and correctly.

I am easily managed. You must merely be firm with me. Show me exactly how you want something done and in a few short lessons, I will do it automatically.

I am the servant of all great men, and alas, of all failures, as well. Those who are great, I have made great. Those who are failures, I have made failures.

I am not a machine, although I work with all the precision of a machine, plus the intelligence of man. You may run me for a profit—or run me for ruin. It makes do difference to me.

Take me, train me, be firm with me and I will place the world at your feet. Be easy with me and I will destroy you. Who am I?

I am habit!

Ahhh! There's the answer. You arrived at your destination safely because you relied on your habits. You learned how to drive a long time ago and had lots of practice to ingrain the technique within you. You had probably driven to this destination many times in the past, and consequently didn't have to think consciously about the route. You just got behind the wheel, set the autopilot and took off.

Who's driving this bus?

You see, as much as ninety-five percent of all our behavior is automatic, unthinking—habitual. You can easily understand how this system works when you are driving a familiar car to a equally familiar destination—but let's take a look at how our unthinking habits impact other aspects of our lives.

It's reported that there are 100 million impulses, which assault the mind every second, carrying information from the body senses. A few dozen are permitted to enter the brain stem and of those, the conscious mind heeds only a few—actually seven—plus or minus two. Right here I begin to see that I am filtering out way more stimuli than I am letting in.

So, for instance, in order for you to read these words and focus on the information contained on this page, you are turning your available attention units to the task at hand. You are relying on your learned habits to take care of many of the other related aspects of this project. There is no conscious thought on how to sit upright in your chair, how to hold the book or turn the pages. So far, this is a pretty good system. And as long as I am willing to live with the status quo and do not aspire for growth and a greater set of results in the world, I'm just fine.

If, however, I want a better quality in the reality of my life, both personally and professionally, then I have to take a different action. I have to start looking at what habits I am engaging in on an unthinking level which assist me in getting my desired results, and more importantly, which actually deter me. As John Dryden said, "We first make our habits, then our habits make us."

Let the games begin

Here's the challenge. We all learned at a very young age, a method for responding to, interacting with and wielding power. We probably didn't call it by name—power—we knew it rather as an experience. Regardless, what we learned in those formative years, is probably operating on some habitual level in our lives right now.

Think about it. As a baby, I have no power in my life. If I get my most basic needs met, it is because some powerful, godlike beings make it happen for me. I learn very quickly that *they* have all the power. Soon, however, I might begin to see a cause/effect relationships between my actions and their responses. I cry—they come running. Ahhh! That feels powerful. I make noises—they laugh. Oooh! I like that, too. I throw my cup across the room. They scowl. Well, I'm not sure I like that face, but there's something neat about the fact that I seemed to have created it.

I'm sure you have seen children acting out in public. They scream, yell, throw things and generally give their parents a miserable time. The parents may issue warnings like, "If you don't stop that, I'm taking you home." They may threaten them with a spanking or any number of other things. All the while, the child continues to wreak havoc.

Haven't you seen that and thought, "Interesting. That child is totally in control of the entire situation." It's odd. The child is getting a negative response, but nevertheless seems to enjoy owning the power in the encounter.

So my questions is—what did you learn about power in your home? In order to decide which of our "Power

Habits" need to be changed, it becomes imperative for us to take a conscious look at what we are doing that works and what doesn't. And it is extremely helpful if we get an understanding of how we learned those behaviors in the first place.

I learned this: If I yelled or became demanding, there would be extreme negative ramifications. I believed that I was totally powerless in most all situations. I also thought that this reality, as I experienced it, was the way of the world. I had no reason to doubt the veracity or the logic of the system.

I also noticed that my mom seemed to have the power most of the time. In a funny sort of way, she acted out like that small child—especially when she was drinking. Our family dynamics, activities and focus would all center around making sure that she wouldn't get annoyed or angry. We all tiptoed around in fear and anxiety, getting as small and insignificant as possible. If she didn't notice me— I might be OK.

When she would stop drinking, a most interesting thing would then transpire. She would become contrite and remorseful, at which point the balance of power would dramatically shift. My dad would then be the one in control. It was the only time in their relationship when he would feel powerful enough to express himself. In a twisted sort of way there was a payoff for him.

What I learned as a player in this power game was simply this. Everyone else had the real power in life. And the only way for me to get any power was to either

1. Disappear (at least this way I had power over my own safety).
2. Stand out and be nothing less than perfect.
3. Manipulate others by giving them what I thought they wanted.
4. Play the victim and hope someone felt sorry enough for me to help me out, and/or

5. When those powerful "others" stumbled, I
should jump on the opportunity to take advantage of the situation.

The unvarnished truth

There it is. That's what I first learned about power and my habitual behaviors came directly out of that learning. Let's see how this showed up later on in my life.

In my personal life, I continually gave away all my power. I wanted so desperately to please that I didn't have a clue as to who I was or what I wanted out of life. Gradually the strategy of disappearing was replaced with the one for being perfect. If I was the smartest, the funniest, and the boldest, I learned I could get your attention. If I was the best cook, interior decorator and seamstress, maybe you would want to marry me and take care of me and I'd never have to contend with that cruel hard world out there. If I was the sexiest, thinnest, blondest and most outrageous dancer—well then, not only would you marry me, but you'd give me all your money and never again look at another woman.

If I was the most selfless, giving, accommodating friend, family member or co-worker, then I would be the most popular, best liked, and everybody would give me everything I wanted in return—only I wouldn't even have to ask for it—they would just know.

Oh please. Does this make you want to barf? It does me. How in this entire life could I *ever* have the slightest true success with those kinds of habitual patterns running the show? And here's the thing, I didn't even know they were habitual patterns! It was just how things were. I was simply doing what I had always done, I was on autopilot heading directly for the side of a mountain with absolutely no consciousness whatsoever.

What happened to me on December 7, 1969, was a logical consequence of my actions up to that point. As I mentioned, when I awoke that morning I immediately slipped into a severe panic attack. The terror and extreme anxiety surrounding my being was overwhelming. I felt totally helpless, powerless and petrified with fear.

I'm going to make a bold statement here. I believe that I reeked "victim." My smell was probably so strong that when Mr. Escaped Convict jumped his guard, grabbed the gun and dashed away, he knew exactly where to run. He just followed the unmistakable odor of an easy mark. Isn't this what happens with animals in the wild? Doesn't the stronger, more powerful animal sense where its vulnerable, weak prey hides?

The good news is that the experience itself served as a screaming, clanging, rattling wake-up call for my consciousness. In the five hours I endured captivity I got the opportunity to stand outside myself and watch my multidimensional thinking and simultaneous realities with a perspective that seemed to cram lifetimes of learning into mere moments.

Obviously, you don't need to experience a life-threatening experience in order to become aware of your habitual patterns of behavior. It can be a shortcut, as it was for me, but it's not a method I would necessarily recommend.

What follows are some ways that you can enter the world of the conscious competent (or conscious incompetent) with less stress. You'll notice that the biggest demand on you at this point will be to force yourself to get out of your comfort zone and start noticing things. Turn off the cruise control and begin to pay attention.

Danger! Danger! It may feel like work. You may want to go right back to the way things were, to the way they've always been. Don't do it. Stay in the process. Each success will build on the preceding one until the uncomfortable actually becomes the comfortable. Also, throughout this book I'll give you strategies to help you overcome those self-defeating behaviors which pull you back to "the way things have always been done."

How to get off autopilot

1. **Hold a mirror up to yourself.** Take an objective look. Here are the guidelines for optimum benefit:

- Get a journal and write down your observations. Make your thoughts concrete.
- Record your earliest memories, conclusions and decisions you made about power.
- Determine how your beliefs and perceptions have shaped your behaviors.
- Answer the following questions: How have those beliefs and behaviors cost you in your business relationships? In your personal life?

2. **Actively solicit feedback.** Ask people for their input on your effectiveness—in various domains of your life. *And*, tell them they have your permission to be totally honest. Remember, if you hear something that you don't agree with, or that causes you an emotional reaction, just breathe, listen and consider their input. A friend of mine once showed up with a button on his shirt that summed it all up. It read, "The truth will set you free. But first it will piss you off." How true.

3. **Notice what works and what doesn't.** If something isn't working—change it—right away. The longer you continue a certain behavior or action, the more ingrained the habit becomes.

4. **Pay particular attention to the *people* in your life.** People you normally walk right by with little more than a flip hello. Really notice them. Give them your undivided attention, if only for a few minutes.

5. **Challenge your assumptions.** Become conscious of your limited beliefs that may have put you in a place of powerlessness. Commit to let them go and replace them with new empowering ones.

If you have always believed, for example, that someone "like you" could only earn "X" amount of money or rise to a certain level in the company, or attract a certain kind of partner or mate, then right now, let that belief go. If you have traditionally held the belief that once you've made your way to the top in your company, the secret becomes how to stay on top. Challenge that belief. Look around you for exceptions to the rule. Become one yourself.

The above five practices will begin the process of re-connecting you with the your true power. They are designed to help you take the very first step which is to get conscious. We cannot move forward in any specific direction until we first acknowledge where we have come from and what beliefs and attitudes have brought us to this particular place. If we do not, we are doomed to repeat the same mistakes again and again—and of course, reap the same results.

In the words of Peter Senge in *The Fifth Discipline*, "the discipline of working with mental models starts with turning the mirror inward; learning to unearth our internal pictures of the world, to bring them to the surface and hold them rigorously to scrutiny."

Say it isn't so

While you are doing these things, it is important to remain "lovingly detached." Sometimes, when we finally become honest with ourselves, we can fall into a state of self-re-crimination and despair. "I can't believe I have been doing this for so long. What an idiot I must have looked like. Why didn't someone tell me?" And on and on.

No. Instead congratulate yourself for finally waking up! Applaud your courage and your commitment. There is HUGE power in being able to own one's "stuff." It no longer controls us—we are now able to acknowledge it and move forward.

Example. One of my real world self-limiting habits *was* (that is, *used to be*) a tendency toward massive disor-ganization. Oh, I had lots of explanations and excuses why everything around me was always so scattered and messy. "I don't have time to straighten it out. It's not all that important. I don't have the right kind of drawers, file cabinets, shelves, blah blah blah."

I now understand that every time I gave one of those excuses, I appeared defensive, rigid and powerless. Once again, I put the power—out there somewhere. For a long time I told myself that the fact that I was so disorganized had no impact whatsoever on my ability to produce. And to that I now reply "bull." If others see me as scattered and fragmented—does that engender trust in my abilities? I think not.

Detach. Observe what you are doing that doesn't work. Decide on a new course of action. Try it. Move through the awkwardness of something different. If it gives you the results you are looking for, great! If not, do something different.

One thing for sure—it is impossible to sleep through this process. You will be compelling yourself to become aware, to make new, more empowering choices and ultimately, to reap greater successes.

Strategy No. 2
Create a Rich, Vivid Vision

I always wanted to be somebody, but I should have been more specific.—Lily Tomlin and Jane Wagner

I love the awareness that everything that exists as a physical reality first started as an idea in someone's mind. Everything in nature started as an idea in the mind of God, and everything which has sprung from the development of mankind started first—as an idea.

You're probably sitting on a chair which some human being first conceived within their mind. You may be inside a house which, once again, lived as a picture in someone's mind long before it became a reality. Imagine the difficulty some people have had selling their ideas when they seemed unreal and others couldn't see what they could see. Examples of this certainly would include electric light, the telephone, the airplane and many, many others.

I remember a story I once heard about a reporter who was at the opening of Disney World. He stood next to someone from the Disney organization and remarked, "Too bad that Walt isn't here to see this." The Disney representative remarked, "Oh but he did see it. And that's why you see it now."

The most powerful people know, quite specifically, what they want. They create a mental equivalent of the thing they desire, a picture which is so rich, detailed and compelling that it literally pulls them toward it. They become motivated and driven by that picture. It acts like a magnet, pulling them forward, enabling them to overcome obstacles and achieve their desired results.

And the rest of us may not know exactly what is going on, but we want to be a part of it. We get caught up in the passion that fuels their vision and we actually begin to see what they see. We, then, become motivated as well.

Exactly what do you *want*, anyway?

Most of us begin with no end in mind. At best we may have this vague idea that we want to end up "happy" or successful" in our lives, but we have never really defined what that means to us—or exactly what it will look like when we have achieved it.

We just kind of shuffle along hoping for the best, compromising our needs and our values. Then one day we find ourselves somewhere we don't want to be and we don't have a clue as to how we got there. We don't quite understand that where we are at any time in our lives is a direct result of the moment to moment choices we make every day. All of our small, seemingly insignificant decisions add up and ultimately become our destiny.

What if we designed our outcome from the very beginning? What if we hung up a picture of what we wanted our lives to look like first and then set our autopilot to that destination? I assure you, if we were lined up on that heading, our day to day decisions would be well chosen, and our results would be dramatically different. We would be the conscious architects of our lives.

I'm sure you know that any airplane in the sky is off course over ninety percent of the time. Things like other aircraft, wind currents and weather systems serve to alter the original course of the plane. The reason the plane arrives safely at its destination is because first it defined, most specifically, its desired result. Then, no matter what obstacles threw it off course, its internal autopilot kept it heading in the right direction by making constant little corrections.

I remember in 1994 when I came face to face with this awareness. I had been working as a communication consultant and trainer in the legal field since 1989. I was in the enviable position of being in a relationship with a man who was winding down his practice as a lawyer and, as a result, he looked forward to more travel and play. That was fine with me. Since we were living a very comfortable life together, I did not actively solicit any new work. I was, metaphorically, on the chaise lounge of life—and quite frankly—I was loving it. Oh yes, there was a nagging little voice inside me that kept asking questions like, "But, Linda, exactly what do you want to create in your life with this man? After being together for fourteen years, do you even know?"

Whenever I heard that voice I would simply distract myself and focus on something else. That is, until Thanksgiving Day in 1994 when I was confronted with reality.

I remember I was standing in the kitchen making coffee. I heard Jim walk up behind me, pause, and then clear his throat. He said, in a somewhat thin voice, "I have something to tell you." I turned and looked at him. When I saw his face, a sinking feeling of dread dropped in over my body. He then said, quite simply, "I do not want to be in this relationship anymore."

It wasn't as if I didn't know this was coming. On many levels, I had been experiencing the same feeling of discontent as he was. Nevertheless, I remember feeling a little detached from my body for a moment. Everything seemed somewhat surreal. It was like someone in the not too distant background suddenly spoke through a large megaphone. The voice barked out, "It's time to get off the chaise. Please move. Your time is up. Someone else needs the lounge."

Talk about powerless. There I was, forty-something years old. No real job or career. No consistent income. No savings. No retirement. No plan for the future. Zip. I was a good fifteen pounds overweight and out of shape (not that big a deal, except that it manifested as hideously low energy). Without going into all the ridiculous details, suffice it to say that it was not a pretty picture and I was scared. Although Jim had provided for me quite nicely while we were together, he had no intention of continuing to do so.

I took my whimpering little self to a friend, coach and advisor whose first question to me was, "Linda, what do you want to create in your life—*apart* from this man?" I had no clue. Not even a vague idea. I could tell him what I *didn't* want. I didn't want to be sad. I didn't want to be financially strapped. I didn't want to be alone. But here's what he pointed out to me about that kind of thinking.

He said that the mind cannot compute a negative. That in order for me to even grasp the concept of *not* being, let's say, sad, I have to call up a picture in my mind of me *being* sad in order to instruct my mind *not* to think of it. And it's not the words that will guide me forth, it's the picture—that vision of sadness that I am holding in my mind. I will subconsciously seek to recreate that picture in reality. He said that it was possible to actually use that strategy to my advantage but first I needed to understand what motivates us to move in any particular direction.

He pointed out that as human beings we are motivated by only two things—the pursuit of pleasure or the avoidance of pain. He said that we can, in effect, get leverage on ourselves by using this awareness consciously.

The pleasure/pain principle

Here's how it works. I may choose to go work out because I want to avoid the pain of feeling sluggish, flabby and overweight—or I may go work out because I want to pursue the pleasure of how great I'll feel afterward—or how I'll feel when I look in the mirror at my lean, healthy body. I might choose to take a course in advanced communications because I want to avoid the pain of possibly failing in my career or because I want the pleasure of succeeding. We're all driven by different things.

This understanding works to give me the motivation to choose a course of action which is in alignment with my vision. It is part and parcel of that vision. It can pull you toward the picture of what you do want—or it can send you running in the opposite direction of what you don't want. Without this awareness, you can end up right smack in the middle of nowhere. Not in enough pain to actually do anything about it, and without the lure of a strong pleasure to pull you forward. This place is known as the "Holding Box." Crabby, miserable, resentful automatons reside here. If you see anything which even vaguely resembles this place—turn and run for your life.

Looking good—feeling great!

I decided that I definitely wanted to create an intensely pleasurable picture to pursue—so I began the process. Mentally I painted a rich, vivid, detailed representation of my life—of me at my absolute finest and best. I included all the domains of my life—personal, family, health, career, spirituality. I used all of my senses as I envisioned myself actually living at this heightened level of joy, fun and passion.

I felt what I would feel if I had already achieved that state of being. I experienced in my mind the excitement, the love, the bliss, the wisdom. I saw how I looked as I achieved this state. I noticed my face—bright, expressive, full of expectancy. I saw my entire body, healthy, energetic, lean and strong. I saw myself spinning and dancing and singing like Aretha Franklin (my idol!). I saw myself surrounded by a healthy, loving, supportive family and lots of dear close friends. I saw myself living with an abundance of resources. I saw myself giving—unconditionally—of my time, my talents, and my wealth to those in need. I could taste, smell, feel, hear and see love—in all its myriad, dimensional, colorful forms. I was immersed in it. I swam in it and became one with it. It tickled me, enveloped me and totally supported me. Oh rich, rich, rich!

You see, by placing this compelling picture of myself out in the front of my consciousness, I was instructing my subconscious to make it happen. And it was a strong lure, indeed. The pull toward the realization of that vision was undeniable. But I was still curious about the other avenue— the one called avoid the pain. I decided to give it a try.

Looking bad—feeling miserable

I will say up front, this one really works. It isn't easy, it doesn't feel particularly good, and in fact, it can be rather painful. It does, however, produce measurable results. Here's what I did.

First, I got clear on what behaviors, beliefs and attitudes I was engaging in on a continual basis, which I knew were self destructive. For instance, in terms of my physical health, I was not eating properly or getting any physical exercise. In the area of my personal goals, when things got tough—I would just give up. If it was too much trouble, why bother? With my partner I remember compromising a lot of my needs in order to make him happy. And even though I knew that I should be taking responsibility for my career and for generating income for myself, I became content to let him do it. After all, he seemed so good at it. And if he wanted me available to zip away and play for a few days here or there, I knew I'd better be available.

By the way, I am in no way placing the responsibility for my choices on anyone but me. He made a request—I complied. End of the story.

In other areas of my life I continued to compromise my values, my needs and my identity in order to please, while simultaneously controlling anything and anyone I possibly could. It's a clever trick to manage both at the same time. Without any conscious endeavor, I was becoming rather adept at it.

With those self-defeating behaviors (and more) honestly laid out, my next task was to take a long hard look at exactly what my life was going to be like in five, fifteen and twenty-five years if I made *no* changes in how I was operating. In other words, if I continued to do exactly what I was doing, specifically how would that manifest itself in my life five years from now? Or fifteen? Or twenty-five?

In this experiment I walked myself out twenty-five years into the future. I was seventy years old. I stood in front of a mirror and here's what I saw.

Since I had never changed my eating and exercising habits, my body was extremely heavy, flabby and sagging. My face looked tired and lifeless. There were dark circles under my eyes. Since I had no income I couldn't afford to take care of any of my personal needs. I was living off welfare checks and food stamps. My hair was gray and stringy. My dress, an extra, extra large loose fitting muumuu, came from the local consignment shop. It was a faded gray, which matched the color of my skin. My fingernails were ragged and unpolished.

I looked around to see who was in my life. Who did I love, who loved me? What were my relationships like? Well, since I had never changed that "Let someone else take care of me" routine—there was *no* love in my life.

Job? Nope. Happiness? None. Friends? You've got to be kidding. Energy? Fun? Passion? Zero. I saw that I was an embarrassment to my brother and my son had disowned me. I had no car, no home and no money. Then when I felt that I had reached the bottom of despair, I added one more inch of leverage—and this is what sent me over the top. I saw myself having to go back to my former lover and ask him if I could borrow money. I can't even describe what that scene was like—except that it was the most humiliating experience of my life. It was profoundly disgusting. Unbearably repulsive. Nauseating and loathsome. I felt like some tragic character in a depressing play.

So I have a tendency to over dramatize a little. But in this case it was extremely effective. I fully associated with the pain. And in that highly emotional moment I solidly anchored in my mind, body and spirit that I absolutely would do *whatever* I had to do so as *not* to end up there. Period. It was as though, up until that moment, I was standing on the down side of a teeter-totter and someone threw a thousand pound rock on the other end. Ka-boom! I was launched! That picture—that vision, if you will, was so crystal clear to me that it was as if it were real. I wanted absolutely no part of it.

I invested in a yearlong training program to learn how to master my life, my health, my finances and my relationships. I joined a health club and began a regular exercise program. I started eating healthy foods. I got exceptionally clear on what kind of loving, intelligent, funny, confident man I wanted in my life. The kind who respected my desire to grow and continue to learn. I started letting go of some of the material things in my life, which up to that point, I thought gave me security. (What an illusion!) I reconnected with the people I loved. I focused every single day on all the things I had to be grateful for—in order to lift my spirits and align myself with what was truly important in my life. I developed a marketing plan and began to actively pursue my career as a professional speaker.

Accordingly, I became extremely action oriented. Whenever I would wake up and not *feel* like working out or mailing out another marketing piece, I would simply play that *Avoidance of Pain* video in my head and I would immediately move forward.

The key to this strategy is that you cannot merely sit back and poke at the images from afar. You must go 100 percent to that future time and fully experience what it will look and feel like if you have changed none of your self-limiting behaviors and attitudes. Again, it doesn't feel particularly good, *and* it is extremely effective.

Looking back now on my kidnapping, I see that this principle was clearly at work. I had created in my mind an overall vision, a picture of myself free, alive, safe and secure. I had set myself up to do whatever was necessary in order to pursue that pleasurable picture. I did not know *how* to consciously create that picture—I didn't need to know how. I just needed to know what.

Give me one good reason . . .

Part and parcel of the picture, the vision, or the "what" is the "why." Friederich Nietzsche once wrote that "He who has a 'why' to live for can bear with almost any 'how.'" The "why" provides the fuel for your mission.

I know that during the time I was held captive I had an extremely compelling reason for wanting to escape. It wasn't just so I could go bowling the next evening. It was something much more powerful than that. It was that I finally understood what was meant by the preciousness of life. I got it—on a visceral level. It wasn't some thought or concept which sounded good. It was extremely, electrically real to me. I felt it. And I wanted it—desperately. I wanted to be with my son and cherish my every moment with him. I wanted a second chance.

The great news is that we don't have to go to hell and back in order to get this awareness. We can get it right now, without all the trauma. Here are some specific strategies to help you harness this power.

Action Ideas

1. Get crystal clear on what feelings you want to create in your life. Joy? Passion? Happiness? Peace? Love? Specifically define those feelings.

2. Ask yourself, "What kind of a life would give me those feelings? What would it look like? How would I be living? What would my relationships look like? What kind of work would I be enjoying? Who would be benefiting from the contribution I would be making in the world?

3. Cut out pictures from magazines that represent your mental pictures and feelings, and post them somewhere you can see them often.

4. Talk about your vision, passionately. You will notice others starting to experience your energy and enthusiasm—which in turn will refuel you.

5. Take consistent action toward that vision. This action step becomes easier and easier as you build momentum and make progress.

It says in the Bible, "where there is no vision, the people perish." I also contend that when we have no vision, we end up following others who do. So I can either decide for myself what I want my life to look like—or get whatever comes up by default.

I encourage you to create your own rich, compelling, vivid, detailed vision. Imbue it with emotion and feeling. Let it work through you, for you and become a reality. Watch as you discover the ways and means to manifest it. Observe as divine right action moves in and provides opportunities you might never have noticed before. Feel the power of that picture pull you forward, unabashedly, joyously and magnificently.

Strategy No. 3

Make Up Your Own Stories

He is in possession of his life who is in possession of his story.
—Carl Jung

There's what happened. Then there's my interpretation and response to what happened. And then—there's how others choose to interpret and respond to my response. The ripple effect doesn't stop there, either. It just keeps on going, perpetuated by people who love the drama, who seem to enjoy being a part of the problem and place the responsibility for the whole situation on something or someone else.

Dr. Stephen R. Covey's first habit in the *Seven Habits of Highly Effective People* is "Be Proactive." He says that anytime you think that the problem is out there, that *thought* is the problem. You have just empowered what's out there to control you. You may not be able to always choose what happens to you in life, but you certainly can choose your response to what happens—and thereby stand fully in a place of power.

My friend, David, has adopted an interpretation of this principle that I have taken on as well. His initial version of his story went like this, "Everything in my life I create, promote or allow." He said as he examined the events, situations and experiences of his life, he concluded that this credo pretty much said it. Then, one day as he was walking his dog, Mac, he had an experience that changed his perspective.

He said as he walked along the sidewalk, he suddenly realized that he had stepped in something and it was all over his good shoes. Apparently someone else had walked their dog along the same path and had failed to observe our local ordinance for cleaning up after your pet. As he stood there looking at the mess, he thought to himself, "Wait a minute. I didn't create this. This is not of my creation. I didn't promote it and I certainly did not allow it."

He said that as he pondered his miserable state of affairs he stumbled across a realization that explained what had happened. And in that moment he changed his theory. From that time forth he espoused the following: "Everything in my life I create, promote, allow . . . or step in."

That's it, isn't it? Sometimes you just step into a bad situation. What will separate you from the ineffective, powerless person will be how you choose to interpret and respond to the situation. I have heard it said that it's not the facts of life that can trip me up—but rather the interpretation I place on the facts.

I know this. After my kidnapping I could have concluded that, just as I had always suspected, the world was not a safe place. I could have decided that the only logical course of action from that point on would be to trust absolutely no one. Never, ever walk alone anywhere. Constantly be looking over my shoulder for the one who was out to get me. Truly, this entire experience could have been nothing more than reinforcement for how I had been thinking up until that day. I don't think anyone would have blamed me for taking that interpretation. I simply chose otherwise.

I decided to believe that in this experience I discovered power and strength I never knew I had. I chose to believe that without that loud wake-up call, I might have actually succumbed to my suffocating depression and taken my own life. I concluded that God always sees the bigger picture and continually chooses life. That I was so loved and supported that I was given the opportunity to expand my consciousness and make a more empowering choice.

As I go through life I am continually finding opportunities to make up stories and subsequent choices which support me in my overall quest—to live a life which is rich, abundant and fun! There is never a day that goes by when I cannot practice the power of choice and proactivity to bring me high-quality outcomes.

We're on an adventure

I remember when my husband, John, and I went on our first vacation together. We were both excited. In the days leading up to and including our actual departure day, he kept saying, "I can't wait to go on vacation. We're going to have so much fun."

The day arrived. We drove an hour and a half to Tampa to catch a plane that would ultimately get us in to Albuquerque a little after midnight. Since the rental car agency in Albuquerque closed at one A.M., this was perfect. However, when we got to Tampa, we discovered that our flight had been canceled. If we waited for the next flight, which was four hours later, it would be too late to pick up the rental car. We decided to get in line to rebook on another rerouted flight.

When we got to the ticketing section of the airport we noticed that the rest of the 100-plus passengers had decided to do the same thing. The line was enormous! I remember John's exasperation was growing. He said, "At this rate we'll never start our vacation." Apparently he was not alone in his frustration. As I looked down the line of waiting passengers, the predominate facial expression was a high-intensity scowl.

As I stood there, I began to think about how I could choose a more empowering interpretation of this event. No, I did not choose this situation. This was rather something I "stepped in." But was I going to allow the situation to have power and control over me? I decided not.

I turned to John and said, "Honey, what if we decided that we are on vacation starting right this very second? I mean, we're not at work. We're with each other. We have no responsibilities whatsoever. We have chosen to interpret this experience as 'bad,' but what if we labeled it instead as 'an adventure'? What would we be doing right now if we were on an adventure? How could we start having fun this very instant? What would we be thinking? What would we be focused on?"

He looked around for a second and then started to laugh. He said, "Well, if we focused on the faces of all these crabby people, that would give us some fun entertainment!"

I laughed and suggested that we get someone to take our picture in front of the crowd so that we could record the experience. We enrolled a nearby gentleman to capture the moment as we turned to the entire line and invited everyone to be a part of our picture. A few people started to laugh. When they did, John looked at me and in his best Mickey Mouse voice said, "People, people, people, people! I just loooooove people!" More people started laughing. A man started singing "It's a small world after all."

Someone in the crowd asked how we could be in such a good mood when everything was going wrong. John's response was, "Ahh, but everything is deliciously right. We are right now, in this very moment on a fantastic vacation. We're on an adventure!"

Now that's just an interpretation, isn't it? We made it up. But look at the effect it had on us—and on others as well! We proactively used our power to choose our response and, accordingly, completely altered our experience. In choosing our response, we were choosing our attitude, weren't we? And attitude is something we bring to life— it's not something we get out of life.

Hone your skills of persuasion

Taking this idea into my workplace I begin to see how my attitude not only impacts my experience, but others as well. Here's where I see the true power of this strategy. Others are affected by the positive energy, which is a result of my choices. And when that happens, my ability to influence and persuade others has heightened dramatically.

And couldn't you use that ability constantly in your professional career? Don't you need to persuade others to listen to your point of view, to join you in a project, to help you when you need it, to buy your product?

Here's a definition of persuasion that someone told me a long time ago. It makes perfect sense to me. Persuasion is transference of feelings. That's it. And your feelings come right out of your interpretation and your beliefs about the subject at hand. If I am apathetic, frustrated, angry or bored about the situation—those are the feelings you will pick up. They will be transferred to you. Odds are, if you don't need or want any more of those negative feelings in your life, you will either reject my offer, or go along with it if you have to, and resent it all along the way.

Enthusiasm—the big payoff

When we choose our interpretations we can select ones that produce an extremely powerful motivator for others and ourselves. That motivator is enthusiasm. Here's what Walter Chrysler, founder of the Chrysler Corporation, says about success.

"The real secret of success is enthusiasm. Yes, more than enthusiasm, I would say excitement. I like to see people get excited. When they get excited, they make a success of their lives. You can do anything if you have enthusiasm. Enthusiasm is the sparkle in your eye, it is the swing in your gait, the grip of your hand, the irresistible surge of your will, and your energy to execute your ideas. Enthusiasts are fighters. They have fortitude, they have staying qualities. Enthusiasm is at the bottom of all progress. With it there is accomplishment. Without it, there are only alibis."

Thomas Edison was enthusiastic about the possibility of creating electric light. His enthusiasm came directly out of his ability to make a different interpretation about what was possible and what wasn't. Other scientists laughed at him, told him he was wasting his time—that there was no future in electric light. Nevertheless, his enthusiasm supported his forward movement. A young reporter once asked him, "Why don't you just give up? After all," he pointed out, "you have tried and failed *5,000 times*." Edison replied, "I have not failed. I have successfully discovered 5,000 ways not to make a lightbulb. I am that much closer!"

Become the author

Here's an idea. Make up some stories about other people.

Wait a minute, Linda. Make up stories about other people? Isn't that what gets us into trouble in the first place?

That depends on what kinds of stories you make up. Do you make up ones that give people the benefit of the doubt? How about ones that make people look good? Do you make up stories about other people that are so positive and compelling that they actually want to step into them?

I remember one morning at 6:00 A.M. when I was in a hotel conference room preparing for a seminar I was to conduct that day. As always, there were lots of last-minute changes: chairs and tables to be shifted around and various and assorted other needs to be met. It appeared that this hotel was understaffed, undermanaged and ill-equipped to handle the demands of the day. A man popped his head in my room and said, "I can't help you now. I'll send William down. And I'm sorry, but, uh, William isn't the greatest. He is, however, all I've got."

As I waited for William to arrive, I thought, "Oh great. Just what I need. A million things to do and I get one of the Three Stooges."

Thank goodness, I suddenly remembered the benefits of making up a more empowering story. I started off by asking myself how I'd be feeling right now if I'd been told that William was simply outstanding and was the absolute best set-up person they ever had. Obviously, I thought, I would be feeling great! And, if I was feeling wonderful, wouldn't that impact how I behaved when William walked into the room? I was certain it would. Then, based on my behaviors, how would William respond? I was curious to find out.

I was ready. I let my made-up story start to work on my head. "Oh boy! I get William! I won't have a thing to worry about since he is so fabulous! I can't wait. No struggles! No strife! All hail, William!"

A moment later, in walks William. Kind of slow. He doesn't say a word. I look at him and my face breaks into a huge smile. "You must be William! I've heard great things about you! My name is Linda and I am thrilled to get to work with you this morning!" I extended my hand.

He stops dead in his tracks. He looks behind him to see if I'm talking to someone else. He finally puts out his hand and mumbles some kind of a greeting.

Now get this. I couldn't help but notice that he was moving *very* slowly. But here's the interesting thing about interpretations and beliefs. When we believe something to be true, we will filter facts through that belief and make them fit. So, if I believed that William was an outstanding worker who appeared sluggish and slow, I would simply justify his actions in accordance with my belief. I thought about it for a moment and then I said, "William, you seem rather tired today. Did you have a grueling day yesterday?"

He responded, "Yes. I worked until one o'clock this morning. I have two jobs."

I stopped what I was doing and proceeded to tell him how impressed I was that he was so committed. I told him that if I had only gotten four hours sleep the night before, I would have probably stayed in bed this morning. I thanked him again for being there and told him that he was making a huge difference in the success of my day, and ultimately for all the people coming to the seminar.

For a moment he looked a little embarrassed. Then he asked if I wanted the pads and pencils put at each person's place at the tables. I thanked him and said that I did.

As he positioned the items on the tables, I noticed that he actually lined the pencils up carefully on the right side of the pads of paper. He also looked to make sure that each setting was an appropriate distance from the next one. At one point I stopped him and remarked that I was impressed with his attention to detail. I told him that a lot of hotel folks just kind of threw the things on the table with no concern as to how it looked. I told him that I very much appreciated the fact that he took such care. I concluded by telling him that he was a credit to this hotel and they were lucky to have him.

It was in that moment that I saw William physically *expand*. He actually became a little taller. He smiled, in spite of himself, and said, "Well, that's my job."

I said, "William, there's a difference between just doing your job and taking pride in it. You have what makes people successful in the world. You are an amazing young man."

I was fascinated by what transpired next. William now began to lay those pads and pencils down with *extreme* care. I think he actually lined up the pencils with all the writing facing up. He even went back and redid the first three or four, because, after all, he hadn't been that careful when he first put them down.

As we continued to work to get the room ready, William did all of his tasks eagerly, with care and with a good attitude. I was extremely impressed. I suppose I was as impressed with the power in my story as I was with William's behavior. I had made up a story that seemed to benefit everyone.

Warning! Beware of the trap!

Did I feel powerful in my encounter with William? Yes, I did. I began to see that I could create the outcomes I desired by using a certain strategy. I also noticed how easy it could be to use the strategy to manipulate others. I could sit around afterward and congratulate myself on what a fabulous job I did. I could justify it by saying, "What's the harm? Bottom line: I got what I needed."

That kind of thinking will ultimately bring me down. First of all, it puts me out of integrity with myself and my values. And when I am not living in alignment with what I believe to be right, the discordance rattles my spirit, my mind and even my physical body. I lose. Secondly, other people will, on some level, pick up the incongruity. It may work at first, but ultimately they will feel used and manipulated. We must line up all of our actions with our highest principles. As Ralph Waldo Emerson said, "Nothing can bring you peace but the triumph of principles."

Your task, at this point, is to take a look at the stories that you have made up in your life which have brought you to where you are now. Do you have stories about how you were raised that explain why you are the way you are? Do you have ones about how you never got the breaks?

Or perhaps you made up a great story about why you can't accomplish that task, or rise to that level or climb that mountain. I assure you, for every thing in your life that you have wanted to accomplish but as yet have not—there are others, with far less resources than you, who have. They just came up with a more empowering interpretation of the facts.

Once you have determined what stories you have created that have kept you stuck, you then get to make up new ones. After all, you made up the original ones in the first place. You just weren't aware at the time that that's what you were doing.

Also practice this. Every time you see a co-worker, boss, friend or family member do something who you judge as "wrong" or "bad," stop. Make up a different story.

Let's say a co-worker comes into the office in the morning, walks right past you and says nothing. Your normal story line might go something like this, "She totally ignored me. She's so rude. She's always doing that." Change it immediately. You could think, "She looks stressed. Something bad may have happened at home. I'll bet she needs some space. She could probably use some kindness, too." *Great story!* It will impact how you feel, which will influence how you behave, which will get you better results in the world.

When Jim and I ended our intimate relationship in 1994, we made a commitment to be friends forever. We both recognized that although it was time to go our separate ways, we could still remain connected on a different level. We swore that we would never let anything keep us from continuing to have a healthy, supportive relationship. It felt absolutely great to me to be able to move forward and at the same time to acknowledge him for all the contributions he had made to me in my life. Accordingly, I took the opportunity to express my appreciation. Not only to him, but to the members of his family—who had also been my extended family for so many years.

What transpired later was interesting. It appeared to me that his new lady friend had a different interpretation of what my expressions of gratitude meant. She may have seen it as an attempt on my part to revive my relationship with Jim—I'm not sure. . . . At any rate, the result of all this was that all communication ended between Jim and me.

So, yes, I was upset by what happened. But later I was able to filter it through an interpretation that worked for me. Perhaps she felt threatened by my relationship with Jim and didn't want him to be reminded of me in any way. I probably would have felt the same way. I wanted to have a friendship with Jim, but obviously that wasn't possible. So be it.

But what I couldn't reframe quite so easily was why, after fourteen years, as the primary father figure for my son, Miles, Jim would terminate his relationship with him. Miles loved him very much. Jim had promised him when we broke up that he would always love and support Miles. Despite the promise, Jim stopped all communication with him, as well.

For a long time all I could feel was anger. I mean, don't mess with my kid. Even though he wasn't a "kid" anymore, I was forever a mom. My anger was growing.

And then one day I heard a story based on *Conversations with God,* by Neale Donald Walsch, which completely changed my viewpoint. Later I altered the story to fit my beliefs.

I believe that as souls we reunite in the space between lifetimes. During this time we are in a place of peace, love and wisdom. All is in perfect order. We decide with Divine Intelligence, what we are going to accomplish, how we are going to expand our capacity to love, and what we are going to learn in the next lifetime. We are beautiful loving souls—unselfishly supportive of each other. We make agreements with each other to provide what the other soul will need.

So here's the story: Before my soul slipped into this body form and personality called Linda, and Jim slipped into his, we were kindred, loving spirits.

One day I said to him, "In the next lifetime, I'm pretty sure that one of the things I need to learn is forgiveness."

His response was, "OK, I can help you with that."

"But how?" I asked.

To which he replied, "I'll give you something to forgive. You have helped me many, many times before, so I will do this for you."

"Oh, wow!" I said. "You've got the hardest job. I know you love me very much. It will be an extremely painful thing for you to do something that would require forgiveness. You're going to have to be the bad guy."

"I'll do it, though. But, please, please, promise me one thing. Promise me that when I am doing that terrible thing, you will never forget who I am and that I love you. Please remember that I am only doing what I promised I would do."

In awe of his selflessness and love, I answer, "I promise. I will never forget."

Let me say that this interpretation totally lifts all anger and resentment out of my being. Is it true with a capital "T"? I don't know. I don't even care. It's true for me, because I say it is and it works 100 percent to put me in a place of peace, power and control over my emotions. And that's the bottom line.

You are the writer of the script of your life. As such, you hold all the power to create exactly the reality that you choose—which leads me to the definition that I hold for power. Power is the ability to choose. The more choices I have, the greater my position of power. People think that position is power. I contend that all positional power gives us—is more choices. How about money? Money certainly gives us power, doesn't it? No. Money gives us, once again, more choices. The mistake we often make is in thinking that we can only get more choices in our life—through some outside source. We already have everything we need to create plentiful, magnificent, rich choices in our lives. It's within us. We simply must name it, declare it as so and use the power. And, I would add, use that power *positively*, for the enrichment of all concerned.

Strategy No. 4

Trust the Unseen Forces
or
Get Out of Your Own Way

The power to move the world is in your subconscious mind.
—William James

"I'm going to hurt myself."

He kept saying those words over and over as he donned his safety gear for the climb. It didn't matter that hundreds of people had ascended the fifty-foot telephone pole before him and returned unscathed. He just "knew" that something bad was going to happen. It also didn't seem to matter that his twenty-five teammates kept assuring him that he would do fine. He just kept shaking his head, proclaiming his dreaded fate. I watched from about thirty feet away with keen interest. I was most curious to see what was going to happen.

As an attendee at Anthony Robbins' Life Mastery seminar in Maui, I was offered, along with the other 1,200 participants, the opportunity to do the Ropes Course. Participants would climb the pole, stand fully upright on the top and lunge across twelve feet to a trapeze swing, which they would grab with their hands. They would then be slowly lowered back down to the ground.

Since I was not scheduled to climb until later on in the week, I decided to spend as much time as possible down at the poles watching other people do it so that I could absorb the most effective techniques. You see, I had lived for many years with a low-grade fear of heights and I knew I needed as much help as I could get if I were to ever get off the ground.

Here's what I had noticed thus far. The participants were tethered to the ground by a wire which was attached to their vest, and ran up above them to a secured pulley system. The wire then came back down to the ground and was held firmly in place by a Hulk Hogan look-alike.

In spite of the comprehensive safety measures, most people appeared simultaneously excited and anxious. Accordingly, most everyone took the trip very slowly. I noticed that if, halfway up the pole, a person looked back down at the ground, he or she would freeze for a while at that level before moving again upward. I also noticed that another place people got stuck was right at the top. It was as if no one wanted to let go of the pole with their hands in order to stand completely upright. Many people hesitated for a long time at that level.

There was a rule, also, that if you went above a certain height, there was no climbing back down. You must continue upward. Again, if you did slip off, Mr. Hulk, who was holding the wire attached to your vest would safely and slowly lower you to the ground. There really appeared to be no actual danger involved in the adventure.

Until I observed this self-proclaimed doomed man, I had made it a point to approach the expert climbers after their successful ventures and ask them how they did it. I asked questions like, "What made it so easy for you? What were you thinking? What techniques or strategies did you use?"

I heard things like, "Don't think about it. Just do it. Don't look back down at the ground. Don't look up. Just keep moving. Trust. Your body knows what to do and how to do it. When you get to the top, simply do the same thing you would do if you were stepping up on the top of a stool to change a lightbulb."

Interestingly, the anxiety-ridden man was hearing a lot of the same advice before he started up the pole. But I noticed he wasn't listening.

Finally he started up the pole. Slowly. Very slowly. He kept looking up the pole and then back down at the ground, his protestations getting louder and more frantic. "I'm going to hurt myself! I know it! I am!"

Finally he reached the "point of no return," about a quarter of the way up. Just above this point, he froze. For thirty-five minutes. He clung to the pole for his very life. His teammates encouraged, coached, pleaded, cajoled. They tried any and everything to get him to move. Nothing worked. Finally the people in charge told him that everything was OK, it was fine for him to come back down. All he had to do was let go of the pole and they would slowly lower him down. That was all. Don't push away from the pole. Simply let go.

He couldn't get it. He kept saying, "But I'm going to hurt myself!" They kept replying, "No, you won't! Just let go. We will lower you down."

Finally, he did the exact wrong thing. He pushed forcefully away from the pole. His momentum then swung him right back in to the pole and he banged his forehead on one of the climbing cleats. He screamed. Those of us watching screamed.

When he was lowered safely to the ground we all ran over to him. It truly was just a scratch, but you would have thought that he had been decapitated. He was now hysterical. "See!" he said, "I told you I was going to hurt myself! I knew it! Didn't I tell you?"

"Gosh," I thought. "What lengths we will go to in order to be right."

But, it was more than a matter of being right. He could have made it successfully up that pole. He had everything he needed to be able to do it. The problem was that he failed to trust himself, his internal wisdom and the power of his subconscious mind. In other words, he got in his own way. And by doing so, he rendered himself power-less.

Issue the best directives

I once heard an analogy of the relationship between the conscious and the subconscious minds which helped me to understand how to use them to my ultimate advantage. It was said that the conscious mind is like the air traffic controller in the tower, while the subconscious can be likened to the pilots in the air. When the controller issues an order to "turn right to a heading of 190 degrees," the pilot does what he has to do in order to make that directive happen. If the controller says, "slow down to 180 knots," again, that's just what the pilot does. The pilot does not debate, argue or reason otherwise. He or she doesn't think things like, "Well, I know the controller said 180 knots—but maybe he meant 150," or, "I know he said to go around again, but he probably was just kidding." The pilot follows the orders and makes them happen. Period.

The same is true of your subconscious mind. When your conscious mind says, "I'm such an idiot," your subconscious mind simply fills the order. It will do whatever it needs to do to make sure that "idiot" happens. When you say "I am successful," your subconscious mind replies, "OK, we'll take care of that."

Your subconscious is a part of the same system that knows how to grow your hair, heal a cut and beat your heart. You don't have to tell it how to do those things. It takes total care of it. Right now, there are amazing systems at work within your mind and body which are keeping this book held upright, keeping you balanced in your chair and focusing your eyes on the words. If you consciously started "trying" to do things you do every day without thinking, you could create a real mess.

I remember once being called up on stage in front of a very large audience. As I walked across the stage I re-member becoming very conscious of my stride. I glanced at my feet, uncomfortably bedecked in spiked high-heel shoes, and noticed that there were thin cracks between the many risers that comprised the elevated stage. "Oh no," I thought. "What if my heel gets caught in one of those thin cracks?"

I am convinced that I thereby issued a directive to my subconscious mind. And sure enough, as I awkwardly jerked across the stage, I firmly planted one of my heels in a crack and walked right out of my shoe. It stayed in the crack and I kept walking. Very attractive.

As I prepared to climb the poles in Maui, I kept repeating to myself, "I know how to do this. Everything I need to be successful in this venture, I already have. I'm on an adventure and this is fun!" The assistant secured the last strap on my vest. I took a few deep breaths and for whatever reason, I still don't know why, I started singing in my head. Music has always motivated and inspired me— so I just allowed it to happen. The song was "Respect" by Aretha Franklin. At that point I laughed out loud. "OK, well I guess I'm supposed to boogie up the pole. All right, I can do that."

As the music started playing in my head I strode confidently over to the pole and without a moment's hesitation, I started up. "R-E-S-P-E-C-T. . . ." Up I went, hand over hand, laughing, singing, continuously moving. My eyes focused on whatever portion of the pole was directly in front of my eyes. "R-E-S-P-E-C-T. . . ." Step, breathe, step, breathe, step, breathe. "Sock it to me, sock it to me, sock it to me. . . ."

All of a sudden, I arrived at the pinnacle. I remember thinking, "OK, Linda. Stand up on top of the stool in order to change the lightbulb." There was a brief moment as I contemplated the fact that I was going to be pushing off with my left foot and stepping on the flat top of the pole with my right. There was a hesitation as I thought, "Is that my dominant foot?" Immediately a voice returned, "Doesn't matter. You know how to do this. Just do it." I promptly placed one foot on the top and as I placed the second one alongside it, I stood completely upright.

What transpired throughout my mind, body and soul in the next two minutes is richly anchored in my memory forever. I looked out over the Pacific Ocean to the surrounding islands, mountains and volcanoes nearby. As I allowed the spectacular beauty of the scene to wash over me, I held my arms straight out to the sides of my body, as if to take more of the entire picture in. I felt as if I was being bathed in a purity and a love that transcended anything I had ever known in my life.

At that point I remember feeling an overwhelming sense of gratitude. I felt so completely blessed and enriched. I stood there thanking God that I had allowed myself the gift of this experience. That I had broken through my self-limiting barriers. That I was here in this amazing place—healthy, alive and aware. I cried and laughed and continued to drink in the magnificence all around me. Finally, I jumped over to the trapeze, firmly caught it in my hands, swung back and forth a few times, after which I was safely lowered to the ground. Henry David Thoreau's words resonated in my mind, "If one advances confidently in the direction of his own dreams, and endeavors to live the life which he has imagined, he will meet with a success unexpected in common hours."

Go with the flow

Even though the experience was over in reality, it lives forever in my soul. I am convinced that my success in this adventure was due to my ability to get out of my own way. There is, indeed, a divine wisdom which flows through each of us. It supports us totally and is ever moving toward wholeness and self-expression. It is life-affirming and it knows how to keep us safe in any situation. You may call this wisdom the Universe, Divine Energy, or the Force. You can call it Fred, if you like. It doesn't really matter. As Shakespeare once said, "A rose by any other name would smell as sweet." In other words what we call it does not change its nature.

For me, it is God. I know that God is working through me, as me. I know that if I am made in the image and likeness of God, then I share in the magnificent qualities of God. God did not make me out of itself and then, after the fact, say "Oh here, let me add some evil, incompetence and stupidity." Of course, because I was given free will and choice, I may elect to use my power to create those miserable states. That's up to me.

Here's my choice now: I know that I have available to me all the power, wisdom and intelligence which is God. As such, I choose to be a channel for that magnificence. I will get out of my own way and allow those qualities to guide my experiences.

When I look back on my kidnapping experience, I *know* beyond a doubt that this was what was at play. I had so many people afterward say, "Oh, I would have fallen totally apart. I never would have been able to do what you did." It was always hard to explain what it was like to feel consciously possessed of a wisdom that had more information than I had, on my human ego level. And the fact is we all have it. We may not believe we have it, but that belief does not alter the fact that it is there.

Outstanding athletes, musicians, writers and performers know it is there. They use it consciously and it gives them enormous power. I remember once watching former basketball great, Michael Jordan, as he literally flew through the air toward the basket. It looked as if he were defying the laws of gravity as he floated in space. I remember thinking that the entire rest of the world could have disappeared and he never would have noticed. His focus and concentration was supreme.

He was in what many people call the "zone," where excellence becomes effortless and time becomes suspended. It is what psychologist Mihaly Csikszentmihalyi calls "flow." It's where we become so absorbed in what we are doing that we become one with it. We have no self-conscious-ness, but are rather in a state of self-forgetfulness.

When we experience that kind of mastery, we are un-concerned with *how* we are doing. We allow none of our attention units to be focused on assessing ourselves. We take every single available bit of attention and place it squarely on the task at hand. Again, we get out of our own way.

I believe that Bruce Barton supported these ideas when he said, "Nothing splendid has ever been achieved except by those who dared believe that something inside of them was superior to circumstance."

How to get there from here

If we are going to live and operate from a place of power in our lives, then it becomes imperative to examine how we can access this internal wisdom. One of the best ways is to learn to quiet our chattering, self-defeating conscious mind so that this intelligence can work through us. The follow-ing ideas will lead us to that flow more readily and easily.

1. **Practice your craft.** Whether you are a mortgage broker or a singer, an investment banker or a golfer, learn the most effective way to do it and practice the techniques until they become automatic and unthinking. Spend lots of time studying others who are already masterful at the task, and find out how they did it. Ask them how they think, what their strategies and practices are, and what their be-liefs are.

A great analogy for this is in the game of tennis. When you are in a practice mode, you are consciously thinking, "OK, racquet back, bend your elbow, step in to the ball. . ." And you do this over and over again. Then, when you are on the court, you drop all that internal coaching and just play the game.

Pablo Casals was once asked by a reporter, "Sir, you are unquestionably the greatest cellist who ever lived. You are ninety-six years old, yet you are still practicing six hours a day. Why?" Casals responded, "Because I think I am beginning to make progress."

2. **Suspend judgment.** Simply observe what works and what doesn't. Instead of berating myself when I miss my mark, I will now merely take note. Did a certain action move me closer to my goal or further away? Was it effective or not? Observe and move forward.

3. **Practice the art of mindfulness.** Go back to the basics. Start paying attention to those aspects of your daily routines which you do without thinking. We frequently attack one task in order to get to the next one, in order to get to next one, in order to get to something we call relaxation or play. For instance we could approach the task of mowing the lawn in one of two ways. The first is to mow the lawn to have a mowed lawn and the second is to mow the lawn in order to mow the lawn. If we mow the lawn as if the act was a nuisance, with our minds somewhere ahead in the future, we are not fully alive during the time we are mowing the lawn. We then do not own that time. We have given it away. Instead practice the art of mindfulness—of being present. I am sure you have heard that "the point of power is in the now moment." That's *every* now moment, including the ones while you are doing something as mundane as mowing the lawn, or walking into your office each morning, or answering the phone or typing an envelope. Practicing this kind of awareness gives you tremendous power. It firmly grounds you and puts you back in the driver's seat of your life. It is also germane to your ability to slip into that altered state where your creative genius can flow through you.

3. **Practice daily meditation.** Spend a few minutes every day sitting in silence. Choose a place where you will not be disturbed. Get comfortable, close your eyes and take a couple of deep abdominal breaths. Simply focus on the sound and feel of your breath as it flows. Don't try to regulate it. Merely let your breath happen by itself. Listen to your mind and notice what transpires. If you find your mind

wandering, bring it gently back to your breath. Whatever happens, it's OK. Just relax and enjoy the process. What you will notice after regular practice is an increased sense of awareness and peacefulness. Your ability to focus on the task at hand will become sharper and more pronounced. Your emotions will be less volatile and you will actually become more productive. Practice at least once a day for ten to twenty minutes.

The above practices will strengthen your ability to trust your inner wisdom and intelligence. They will help you tap into what is already present within you, standing ready to assist you no matter what the challenge or the obstacles. They will bring you increased focus, clarity and confidence. They will help you access the power within.

I conclude with a mantra, of sorts, which I created to help keep me anchored in this reality. I repeat it to myself over and over—especially in times of stress. It goes like this, "God is in me, as me, being me—and I am safe."

And so are we all.

Strategy No. 5

Make Lots of Good Impressions

*A human being is a part of the whole, called by us "Universe,"
a part limited in time and space. He experiences himself, his
thoughts and feelings as something separated from the rest—a
kind of optical delusion of his consciousness. This delusion is a
kind of prison for us, restricting us to our personal desires and to
affection for a few persons nearest to us. Our task must be to free
ourselves from this prison by widening our circle of compassion to
embrace all living creatures and the whole of nature in its beauty.*
—Albert Einstein

During the time I was held captive I had my first real experience with systems thinking—although at the time I didn't know it by that name. I remember every thought of escape played out full circle in my mind, at computer-like speed.

Several hours into the adventure, I began to realize that any hope for survival depended on my ability to slowly convince my captor that I really was very much like him. I set out in very subtle and curious ways to establish rapport with him—a bit challenging when one of the two people involved is brandishing a gun. Nevertheless, I knew it was the correct strategy.

So out of that overall objective, I began to calculate sub-strategies. And here's the interesting thing. I never evaluated any action without taking it around a loop to see where it could ultimately lead.

As the hours passed, it became obvious that, although he was still skeptical, he began to let his guard down a little. His plan was to wait until dark and then take me out of the state. Because of that I knew I had plenty of time to lay my groundwork. I made casual statements about how I wished I had his courage. I told him that I was fed up with my life as it was and that this was perfect for me. I could now finally leave and no one would blame me. He talked about his childhood abuse—I mentioned mine. At one point I remember telling him that I was terrified of guns. That might seem like a pointless thing to say—but again, every single word was a carefully chosen piece of a circle.

A perfect example of the systems thinking process occurred at one point about three hours into the experience. After a brief silence, he turned the gun around, held it by the barrel and handed it to me.

"Here take it," he said.

In the one second it took me to answer, here's what went on in my head.

"Oh my God! He's handing me the gun. This could be my opportunity to escape. OK, so let's say I take the gun. Then what? Do I then point it at him and say, 'Ah ha! I've got you now?' What if he put some sort of safety catch on the gun and rendered it lame? He would then know that I have been lying all this time. Then he would surely kill me. And if he didn't put some sort of safety on it, and I could shoot the gun, could I actually *kill* another human being? Even if I have all the justification in the world, could I do it? Could I stand here and watch him bleed to death? Could I live with that forever? No. No, I couldn't. OK, what if I reinforce how afraid I am of guns and tell him I don't like to even touch guns. What about that? Play that one out. Well, he would then have even stronger evidence to believe that I was, indeed, telling him the truth. His trust level would go higher and his guard would go lower and my opportunity for escape would be stronger."

One second after his words, I responded, "Don't give me that thing—I told you, guns scare me." And from what I read in his eyes, I concluded silently, "Right answer."

Do you see what I did? I played out every action, every "cause" to see its effect. What I noticed then was that *that* effect then became the next cause—which created another effect—which created another cause. And on and on and on. And they did not merely occur in a straight line, they branched out like spokes on a wheel.

The problem in life is that we see things, people, situations as fixed rather than dynamic. We focus on a linear, flat system of change rather than the interrelationships involved. Life really is comprised of circles, all interrelating with each other. When one aspect of one system takes an action—the ramifications are far reaching—which then sets up a new set of dynamics. When we are unaware of or ignore this truth—we have just rendered ourselves powerless in the overall system.

I am also suggesting the following: Everything that moves energy impacts the system(s). Everything.

We can no longer sit back and say, "Well, I didn't have anything to do with *that*." Certainly we have all heard that if we are not a part of the solution, we are a part of the problem. Let's take that idea into our quest for more power in our lives. Let's take a closer look at how our actions impact the system.

The Law of the Conservation of Energy

This law of physics states that energy cannot be created or destroyed, it merely changes form. My energy, in the form of my action, makes an impression on the fabric of life—the system, if you will. It is as if I reach over to a big clump of Play-Doh and I press my thumb into the matter. The imprint stays. I have made an *impression* which not only remains, but forever alters the next formation.

So here's the question. What *impressions* are you making in the fabric of this life? And have you ever considered the impact of those impressions on others? You are so incredibly powerful! You have the ability to profoundly impact other people. And here's the interesting situation: You can wield that power in a positive fashion, for the good of the entire system—or you can use it negatively, without regard for the impact. We sometimes delude ourselves into thinking that what we don't know can't hurt us.

But we are a part of the system! If I pour toxic chemicals into my backyard, I have adversely affected the ecosystem that supports me—and you. If I hurt you, I hurt myself! When I commit an act of aggression upon someone else, I have injured some part of myself, as well. I am not being clever when I "get you back" for something you did. I am rather, picking up a knife and jabbing it into my own hand.

I once heard it said that resentment is like drinking poison—hoping the other person will die. Good analogy.

So—what do you think?

Let's take this one step further. We not only impress the system with our actions. We do it with our thoughts.

I can hear you thinking, *Now wait just a minute. Are you trying to say that I can't have my own private thoughts?*

Well, you certainly can have your private thoughts. My contention is that they simply may not be as private as you would like. And they most assuredly affect others.

Have you ever seen a stranger, let's say a woman, across a room at a gathering and, without even speaking to her, you decided within a few short moments that you either liked or disliked her? You didn't know why—you didn't have any concrete evidence to explain your feelings, it was just something you knew. She made an *impression* on you, didn't she? Could it be that the way that person *thinks* has an influence on you? I believe it does. And, in terms of *your* thoughts—how are they influencing and impacting you—and others?

According to quantum physics, your thoughts are actual matter. There is a scientifically measurable connection between the thoughts we think and the neurological and physiological responses they create. Strong, vivid mental images exert influence over our creative self and have a powerful impact on our bodies as well.

Here's what happens as we turn our thoughts into pictures. The image that we create in our mind exists as a three-dimensional object which, of course, is not actually in the brain. It is rather a by-product of the brain's electrical and chemical reactions. It is composed of electromagnetic wave forms that possess energy and matter. The more emotion and sensory detail involved in that thought, the greater the electrical force it will create, the stronger the resultant energy field, and the more it will mimic reality.

The law of electromagnetic energy is a principal which says this: Whenever we create an electrical energy field, we simultaneously produce a strong electromagnetic field. That field will begin to attract other forces in the outside world to us compatible with that image.

So for just a moment let's look at how powerful our thoughts are. Here's a list of some things which might have occurred to you that support this idea.

- You move to the phone to call someone at the exact moment that it rings. That person is on the other end of the line.
- You and a friend or loved one come up with the same idea at the same time.
- You look at someone and you just "know" what they are thinking. And it turns out that you're right.

The critters have it

I believe this phenomenon can definitely be seen in the animal kingdom. In Rupert Sheldrake's book, *Dogs That Know When Their Owners Are coming Home and Other Unexplained Powers of Animals*, he cites examples of animals who clearly picked up information and did things that can't be ascribed to chance. He talks about cats that disappear just before their vet appointments, and lost dogs that cover hundreds of miles to get to their owner's new home.

I have definitely experienced this with my animals. When I am getting ready to leave my house, whether to simply run to the store or leave for a business trip, my two dogs become hyperactive. They whine and cry as they do when they want to go with me. Now, I will have done nothing blatant such as jingle my car keys or pick up my purse. In fact, my dogs are not even inside pets! They live outside in the yard and on the lanai. Yet somehow they pick up my energy.

I also have a cat who loves to sit around in the kitchen waiting for me to decide that he can have some people food. He will sit there on the floor following my every move. And I swear to you, when I *think* to myself, "Oh, all right. I'll get him a piece of turkey," he leaps up, meows at the top of his lungs and runs to me.

Cats and dogs aside, let's look at the world of people. Here's a stunning example of this phenomenon in action.

During the period of time that I was writing this book, my thoughts were predominantly on it. My excitement was mounting. Since I had decided to self-publish I contacted a book packager who gave me a good price on putting everything together for me. It was a good price—however, it was not a sum of money that I could immediately put my hands on without going into savings or liquidating an asset. Since I had never let not having the money stop me from doing what I wanted in the past, I wasn't about to start now. I made the decision to find a backer. My predominant thought, with all of the accompanying emotional energy, was on finding someone to finance my project.

I began to mention the project to several people. I never made a request, I just started placing the intention out in the world. I let my excitement about the project speak for itself.

Within a week of making the decision to find a backer, and with only one chapter of the book actually written, I met a young man named Chris. He was the new love of my dearest friend, Karen. The two of them had decided to meet my husband and me at a resort in Central Florida, for a leisurely dinner. Within a minute of meeting him, I knew he was an outstanding individual. I liked him immediately. To use my principle here—he had great energy.

We had not been together more than a short time when the subject turned to my book. I said that I was excited about the project and that I was looking for a backer to provide "x" dollars.

As I said the words, I knew what his response was going to be. I knew that he was going to offer his support. When I finished my statement, he commented without any hesitation whatsoever, "I'll back you. When do you need a check?" I could hardly contain my excitement.

Interestingly, when I later mentioned this experience to my husband, he remarked, "I knew it, too! I don't know how I knew—I just felt it. As you were mentioning the book, I could almost feel him formulating his response."

Thoughts are palpable. They are real. They leave impressions in the world. Those impressions become our reality. Perhaps it's time that we become conscious co-creators of our reality by wisely and carefully choosing our thoughts.

Action ideas

1. For the next twenty-four hours, observe your thoughts. Notice what they look and feel like. Are they positive, supportive and affirming of yourself and others? Then that energy is what you are contributing to the fabric of life. Are they negative, resentful and judgmental? Then, likewise, those "droppings" are littering up your physical and nonphysical reality. Just notice what you are putting out. Suspend any self-recrimination at this point. Rather, decide to make a new choice. When you find those negative "autopilot" thoughts returning, simply nudge yourself lovingly back on course by releasing the old and reaffirming the new. Silently repeat, "I get back what I give out. I choose to give love. I choose to give love."

2. Take continuous affirmative *actions*. Here are a few:

- If, while walking down the street, you notice a piece of trash lying on the sidewalk, pick it up and toss it in a garbage can.
- When you see someone doing a good job—tell him or her that you noticed.
- Take every opportunity to hold open a door, give a smile, lend a hand, applaud an effort.
- Send a card to a friend you haven't seen in a while.
- Visit a nursing home. Read stories to the residents. Give hugs.
- Share freely—of your love, your time and your support to those less fortunate.
- Make other people feel important by giving them your full attention.

3. Take loving care of your mind, your body and your spirit. It is a gross contradiction of intention to treat others well—and yourself poorly. You are, indeed, a spiritual being having a human experience. It becomes imperative that you take outstanding care of the vehicle in which you propel yourself through this lifetime. You simply cannot feel or act from a place of power when you have no energy or clarity of thought.

As you begin to change the way you are thinking and acting, you begin to notice a profound shift in the way you are feeling and the results you get in the world.

- As you consciously choose your thoughts, you feel more grounded and you make even more empowering choices.
- As you seize opportunities to give love, you feel more loving and other people begin to treat you more lovingly.
- As you give of your time and energy, you feel more compassionate and other people become your greatest raving fans.

Here comes the trap again

As you begin to live with the thoughts and actions that support the world around you, you'll notice that indeed, you become more powerful. As you put out sincere, loving, positive energy, you observe that you get the same back—compounded. Since you are so quick to help others, they want to help you. Since you give so freely of yourself, people want to give to you as well. People want to do things for you. They love you. They would go to the ends of the earth for you. They become your greatest fans. Herein lies the danger. Your intentions may start to shift.

Again the words of Gary Zukav, "When energy leaves you in any way except in strength and trust, it cannot bring back to you anything but pain and discomfort. An authentically empowered human being, therefore, is a human being that does not release its energy except in love and trust."

Reducing it to its simplest terms, I give love and support to others because it is the right thing to do. It is right action. I don't look for the power it will give me in return. I give, and walk away.

I also continually monitor my intentions. What are my reasons behind any action? Am I doing what I do primarily because I will make a lot of money at it, or am I doing it because many others will be benefited by my actions? Getting compensated monetarily may be a delightful by-product of my actions, but when it becomes the primary reason, my energy shifts dramatically. Other people pick up that energy. I suspect that your customers (internal or otherwise), may not be particularly eager to help you make a lot of money off them. They may be most willing, however, to let you help them meet their needs and make their lives better.

Bottom line: We are an integral, vital, important part of the whole. Our very breath impacts the entire system. From this moment forth we choose correct, right, loving thoughts and actions. We love. We give. We forgive. We trust in this glorious, interrelated, powerful system.

Strategy No. 6

Be a Solution Provider

In order to solve a problem, we must rise above the level of thinking that created the problem.—Albert Einstein

There are many people who, after unsuccessfully trying to accomplish a certain task, will merely throw their hands up in despair proclaiming, "Well, I tried. Obviously, it just can't be done." They look at the challenge (and sometimes at life itself) through a very narrow window and, because they can't see any immediate solution, they conclude there *is* none.

Once again, people have relinquished their power to outside forces. They've abdicated, given up and rendered themselves impotent. They've become powerless in the eyes of others, but most importantly, within their own self-image. Quite simply, if I cannot come up with answers to the challenges before me, I cannot position myself as an effective leader within my field or industry. Effective leaders know how to find answers, for themselves and for their customers.

In this chapter we are going to explore creative ways to find solutions. But before we do that, let's examine the method by which we usually approach most "problems."

First of all, we call them "problems," which sets up a negative physiological response in our minds and bodies. We get tense, anxious and constricted in our thinking when we just hear the word. So, let's drop that terminology. Call them challenges, glitches, minor snafus—anything you want, just eliminate the "p" word.

Ask a better question

As we go through our daily lives we are in a constant state of asking and answering questions. We may not be consciously aware of this, nevertheless, it's exactly what we are doing. If you decide to get lunch, that decision is probably in response to the unspoken question in your mind, "Am I ready to eat yet?" or, "Was that a hunger pain I felt?" If you stop and listen, you'll hear lots of questions going on in your mind. Things like, "How could I possibly solve this difficult problem?, "Could I afford that car?" or, "Why would they ask me to be a part of that project when they can get *her*?"

The interesting thing is that we will pull up answers only to the questions we ask. We won't access answers to unasked questions. And, the answers we do access come only from our frame of awareness and past experiences.

I remember once working with a friend who helped me understand this concept on an experiential level. I was at a stagnate point in my business wherein I couldn't seem to generate the amount of business I needed to meet my goals. I remember saying, "I just don't know what to do to make it happen."

He then asked me a most interesting question. He said, "OK, I know you don't know what to do. But if you *did* know, what would you do?"

I looked back at him and said something truly intelligent such as, "Huh?"

He asked again, "I know you don't know, but if you did know, what would you do?"

I chuckled and said, "Well, like I said, I don't know."

Undaunted, he replied, "Oh, I totally understand, you don't know. But if you did know, what would you do?"

I looked at him and thought to myself, *Oh no, I have a mad dog on my pant leg*. I knew I had to come up with something or I'd be there all day. I started searching my brain.

After a few moments I said, "Well, I guess I could search around for some kind of software that helps people generate business."

He smiled and said, "Cool. What else could you do?"

I missed the ball he tossed back to me. I responded, "Well, I don't know what else I could do."

As he opened his mouth to speak I silenced him with my hand. "OK, OK, but if I *did* know what else to do, what would it be? I guess I would call the National Speakers Association and get a list of all the archived talks other speakers have given on how to build your business."

"Great!" he commented. "What else?"

"Well. I could go through all my old files and contact clients from several years ago."

His eyes sparkled. "Excellent! What else?"

You get the point. I actually sat there and generated a plethora of ideas on how to handle my challenge. But it's clear to me that I would not have, if I hadn't been forced to ask a better quality question—one that helped me access answers.

Is there something in your life that you have deemed "impossible" to do? If so, try asking yourself a better question. Something like, "I know this is impossible to do, but if it weren't what would be my first step?" And then, keep asking the question.

Ask some *dumb* questions

Not only does asking better quality questions lead you to better quality answers, so does asking dumb questions. And most specifically, this technique helps us combat the "because this is the way we've always done it" mentality.

Listen to the words of management expert Tom Peters:

"Mostly, it's the dumb, elementary questions followed up by a dozen even more elementary questions that yield the pay dirt. Experts are those who don't need to bother with elementary questions anymore—thus they fail to bother with the true sources of bottlenecks buried deep in habitual routines of the firm labeled: 'We've always done it that way.' "

Have you ever wondered why bathroom countertops are thirty-one inches high? Industry standard? Well, if you're like me, you probably never thought about it. That's just the way it's always been, right? Let's look a little closer.

About ten years ago I was remodeling the home I was living in. When we got to the master bathroom, my partner at the time, suggested that we raise the height of the counter by eight inches. His reasoning was that since he was tall, about 6' 3", he wouldn't have to lean over so far over the sink. It made sense, but I couldn't get over the feeling that this wasn't the way it was "supposed" to be. I mean wasn't there a legitimate reason that counters were thirty-one inches high?

I researched the matter and I couldn't come up with any logical reasoning. Everyone I asked said, "Oh that's industry standard. It's always been like that." But I wanted a reason, and since I couldn't get one from anyone else, I made up one. I'm not saying this is true, but it could explain a few things.

Think back to the time when mankind first created a space designed specifically for ablutions. Perhaps it was just a small table with a bowl and a pitcher of water. Whatever it was, you can be sure it was a long, long, long time ago. So long ago, in fact, that human beings were quite a bit shorter than they are now.

So here we have an average person, about five feet tall, standing in front of a bowl on a table that is thirty-one inches high. In order to wash up they don't have to do much more than kind of lean forward slightly and their face is very close to the bowl. This makes sense. It's comfortable and logical.

Fast forward through the years. Man gets taller. The height of the table stays the same. The table turns into a counter with a recessed sink, still thirty-one inches high, but man just keeps on growing. Pretty soon we've got a 6' 3" man bending at a 90-degree angle at least twice a day to brush his teeth. And we wonder why so many of us have back problems?

OK, so like I said, I made that up. But it could explain a lot of things. Bottom line is this. What may have been a very good reason at one time, today no longer applies.

The question now becomes, where are the bottlenecks in your personal life and in your workplace? What practices have you been engaging in just because that's the way you've always done it? Practices that may not be particularly effective, but are extremely habitual?

I worked with an attorney once and asked him to consider asking himself some of these dumb questions. He called me several weeks later and said that he had discovered something great in the process. He went back to work and asked himself a really dumb question. He asked himself why he always sat *behind* his desk and his clients sat *in front* of the desk. His only answer was, as you might expect, "Because that's the way it's always done." Right then he made a different choice. He decided to sit on the same side of the desk as his clients.

He said that in the ensuing meetings he felt rapport was established much more quickly with clients. He also reported that they seemed to open up and communicate more easily. He very much liked his new arrangement and was not returning to the old way.

Generate a boatload of ideas

If we plan on getting one or two good ideas that will solve our challenge, we need to first generate a whole lot of possible ideas. From that boatload of ideas we can then dump out the ones that don't work and keep the ones with the greatest possibilities.

I learned the value in this concept firsthand when I was trying to generate a new cover for one of my brochures. When I asked my assistant to come up with an idea, she hesitated, and then finally said she'd try. When I asked about her hesitation, she said, "Well, I don't know if it will be good enough." I told her not to worry, that I was sure it would be fine. I told her to take as much time as she needed. One week later there was still no new brochure design.

The following week I told her I had a great idea. I asked her to take about two hours, find a quiet space without any interruptions, and generate ten possible brochure designs. At first she looked at me like I had lost my mind, but when she realized that I was serious, she got up, gathered her materials and left the room. Sure enough, in less than two hours she came back with fourteen possible designs. Fourteen! Yes, most of them were not usable, but there were at least three that I was excited about. One we actually used.

Question. How was she able to come up with fourteen designs in two hours when she couldn't come up with one in seven days? I asked her. She said that when she was supposed to come up with *one* idea, she felt it had to be perfect. The pressure of that thought kept her from moving forward. But when she knew she had to do so many in such a short period of time, she assumed they couldn't all be perfect. She said she gave herself permission to create some bloopers. She also said that when she started playing with ideas on paper, the actual act of drawing things out stimulated new ideas as she went along.

Why don't you use this technique? Whenever you are looking for any kind of a solution in your life, ask yourself the following question, "What are ten possible solutions to this challenge?" Ask that question of yourself and of those around you. Ask questions, such as, "What are ten ways we could get our product to our customers in half the time?" or "What are ten ways we could improve our office morale?"

Referring back to my day of drama in 1969, I can assure you that my brain was generating your basic boatload of ideas. I could not have afforded to rely on only one possible idea for escape. I merely sat on the sidelines and watched the possibilities spewing forth. All I had to do then was grab the one (or ones) with the greatest potential.

Encourage possibility thinking in yourself and others

This one *sounds* good. Here's how it works. We all sit around and brainstorm ways to produce our desired outcome. Everyone feels free to throw out all of their ideas, even if they sound silly. And each time someone does toss out an idea, everyone nods their heads in approval and applauds. In this system we generate lots and lots of ideas to examine later. Then we get to select the ones we like and explore their feasibility.

Ahhh, but that's not the way we learned to do it when we were growing up. In school we were told to come up with the *one* and only one *right* answer. And when you were called on in class, you had better have it. If you didn't, you probably felt humiliated because you were *wrong*! You learned—either have the one right answer or keep your mouth shut. Whatever you do, don't risk looking foolish. (See Chapter 7 on Looking Good and Being Right).

I'd love to say that as adults, we've all gotten past that mentality. The fact is, however, that most of us haven't. It still feels terrible when we offer a suggestion to someone and they look at us as if we had just thrown up on their oriental rug. We hate it! So what we have to do is make a safe place for people to play with ideas, to say whatever pops into their minds. We have to encourage people to takes risks, have fun and be like a kid again. And, of course, we have to give ourselves permission to do the same.

Comedian George Burns once said, "The genius of life is to be able to take childhood into old age." Great idea! It is reported that at age five, ninety-eight percent of us are highly creative. By the time we are eight years old only about thirty-two percent are highly creative and by the time we are forty-four, the number drops down to two percent! What happened? Well, we became adulterized, that's what happened! Let's compare:

Children (age five)	Adults (age forty-four)
• Take risks	• Play it safe
• Are curious—ask sixty-five questions/day	• Already know the answers—ask only six questions/day
• Have high energy	• Tire easily
• Are action oriented	• Would rather watch from afar
• Find lots of things funny (laugh 113 times per day)	• Are always asking, "What's so funny?" (laugh eleven times per day)
• Are positive	• Find lots of things "wrong"
• Think they can do anything	• Doubt their abilities
• Are self-assured	• Lack self-confidence
• Are aware and observant	• Are on autopilot most of the time
• Are highly creative	• Don't feel or act creative

I know these are generalizations and we will always find exceptions, but it does point out the obvious. If we want to be more creative, we've got to reacquaint ourselves with the qualities we all had as children. We've got to take a few more risks, get more aware, most importantly, have a lot more fun!

Laugh it up!

Here's why. Laughing makes us more creative. It's that simple and it's proven. Alice Isen, of the University of Maryland, confirms it in an article she wrote for the *Journal of Personality and Social Psychology*. She describes a study wherein two groups of college students watched two different videos and then attempted to solve a range of creative problems. The first group watched a funny video of TV bloopers. They probably laughed and chuckled their way through the entire experience. The second group watched a math video titled—are you ready for this—"Area Under a Curve." Ooooh, sounds fascinating doesn't it?

Results: The students in the first group, the "laughers," were found to be 300 to 500 percent more likely to come up with solutions to the problems they were given.

Bottom line: Laughing makes you more creative!

It's not a beauty contest

In the idea generation phase, when we are trying to come up with possibilities, we want to be playful and make it safe for people to express *all* their ideas. We want to create a space and mentality that says, "Give us your tired, your poor, your brilliant, your so-so. Give us all of them! We can evaluate them later, just give us a lot to choose from."

Here's a way to do just that and to have lots of fun in the process. Charles "Chic" Thompson wrote a fabulous book called *What A Great Idea* and in it he identifies what he calls Killer Phrases. He defines them as "A knee-jerk response that squelches new ideas, most commonly said by bosses and government officials." He also calls them a "threat to innovation." They are things like:

- "We tried that before"
- "It'll never fly"
- "Yes, but . . ."
- "The boss will NEVER go for it"
- "If it ain't broke don't fix it"
- "Put it in writing"
- "We've always done it THIS way"
- "It's not in the budget"
- "Don't rock the boat"
- "Get a committee to look into that"
- "You can't teach an old dog new tricks"
- "That's not in your job description"
- "You've got to be kidding"

You can probably think of others. Chic suggests that we can diffuse those Killer Phrases in a variety of ways.

One way is to make everyone in your organization aware of a) the fact that they use them and b) how they stifle our creativity. Another way is to publish a list of the Killer Phrases. Actually get your people to contribute to the list. Put the list up where everyone can see it. Make it "against the law" to use them at work—especially in a brainstorming session.

You could start a brainstorming session by declaring that your space is "off limits" to Killer Phrases. Tell everyone you're aware that they probably won't use any of them (point to the large poster on the wall with 100 of them listed), but suggest that just in case someone forgets, you have a plan. Hand out paper sacks filled with wadded paper or Nerf balls and instruct everyone if they *should* hear one of the verboten sayings, they may bombard the offender with one of the soft, head-safe weapons.

Another way to do this is with money. As everyone enters the room, give each of them ten one-dollar bills. If someone uses a killer phrase, the first person who points it out collects a dollar from the guilty party.

These practices insure the following:

- More ideas will be generated.
- More laughing will occur.
- The people who are frequent users of creativity-stifling sayings will become aware of what they are doing.

Action ideas

In order to become a solution provider, remember these idea-producing actions:

- Whenever you hear yourself saying, "I don't know" counter with, "OK, I know I don't know. But if I did know, what would I do?"
- Start asking some dumb questions.
- Post a card on your desk that says, "What are ten solutions to my challenge?" Remember to ask it often, of yourself and others.

- Publish a list of Killer Phrases (see www.whatagreatidea.com for more info).
- Lighten up! Institute humor programs in both your personal and professional life. Here are a few ideas:
  - ☞ Have a karaoke day at the office.
  - ☞ Hang a punching bag in the break room and paste pictures of senior executives on it (make sure you have their buy-in!)
  - ☞ Create a Laugh-a-bunch-lunch group. Once a month take your entire team to lunch. Each person is to bring three jokes, suitable for mixed company. Everyone votes on the best joke. Winner gets their lunch paid for by the rest of the group.
  - ☞ Have a costume day.
  - ☞ Let your kids be the parents for an entire day. They get to tell you what to do, what to eat and when to go to bed.
  - ☞ Walk backwards around your block. When the neighbors gawk at you, simply smile and say "Hi" as if this was the most normal thing in the world to do.

Make your own list. The important thing is to do activities every single day that make you and those around you laugh. There is huge power, creativity, fun and good physical health in laughter—and in being able to come up with solutions!

Let's conclude, as we started, with the wisdom of Albert Einstein: "Imagination is more important than knowledge. Knowledge is limited; imagination encircles the world."

Strategy No. 7

Build Strong Relationships

Learning how to develop and maintain superior relationships can do more for your career and for your personal life than perhaps anything else you can accomplish.—Brian Tracy

We need other people in this life. In our professional lives we need them to help us accomplish our goals and career objectives. We need them in the form of co-workers, customers and vendors. In our personal lives we need other people for love, support and companionship. These are our family, our friends and our lovers. It stands to reason that better quality relationships equal better quality lives.

Can you think of a friend in your life with whom you have a great relationship and for whom you would do *anything*? For me such a person would be my friend, Karen. I call her KZ. Although we don't live in the same state, and I may not have seen her in a while, I am certain that if she called me and asked for my help, I would be there in an instant. No questions asked. No matter what the situation, as long as it was legal and moral, I would do whatever I could. The bottom line here is that she has a lot of power with me, doesn't she? How did she get it? And those people in your life for whom you would do anything, how did they get that kind of power with you?

As I look at KZ, here's what I see. She is extremely loving and kind. She is a fabulous listener. She is always first to ask me how things are going with me and sincerely eager to hear my response. I also know, beyond a shadow of a doubt that if I needed her for any reason, she would help me. No matter what the situation, she allows me to express myself without passing judgment on my thoughts, feelings or actions. She makes me laugh. She thanks me and acknowledges me when I do anything for her, no matter how trivial it might have seemed to me.

And here's a big one: She thinks I am great! She's one of my greatest raving fans! And accordingly, I have become one of hers. I mean, after all, if she thinks I'm so brilliant, then she must be an incredibly wise woman and an astute judge of character.

The KZ Strategy

If I want to have the kind of power that KZ has, then I must be willing to give what she gives. I must model her method for attaining power. I must closely examine what I call the KZ Strategy.

But first, let's define some terms. Lest the words "attaining power" or "strategy" give you cause to hesitate, let me assure you the intentions behind her actions are not to get power "over" other people. I am using the word strategy interchangeably with practices or habits. Simply said, I want to know what is she doing, how is she thinking and, most importantly, *what are her intentions*? What follows are four practices she engages in which I believe give her the power she enjoys with me and with others. We will find ourselves in that place of power when we learn to:

1. Let go of past garbage.
An old Zen story tells of two monks who were walking by a river at daybreak in the early spring. Because of the melting snow, the river level was high above its banks and totally covered the local footbridge. A young woman in a silk dress stood helplessly by the rushing water, afraid to try and cross on the submerged bridge. She looked pleadingly at the monks. Without a word, one of the monks picked her up, held her firmly above the water, struggled

across the raging water and finally set her down on the other side of the river. He returned back to his companion, and without a word they continued along their journey until sunset when their vows allowed them to speak.

The second monk angrily confronted his friend. "How could you have picked up that woman? You know we are prohibited from thinking about women, much less touching them. You are a disgrace to our entire order."

"Honorable brother," replied the first monk, "I put that woman down on the other side of the river at sunrise. It is you who have been carrying her around all day."

What past hurt, anger and resentment have we been carrying around for years like so many bags of heavy garbage. It's time to let it go. It simply does not serve us and it puts us in a place of total powerlessness. We are using up too many valuable attention units and we are only hurting ourselves.

The KZ philosophy? No need to hang on to anger. They were just doing the best they could at that time in their lives.

2. Freely share . . .

- Your time. My first thought when I pondered how well KZ does this, was, "Well, she must simply have extra time in her life. I, however, do not." Upon closer examination I realized that she had no more "extra" time than I did. She simply made helping other people a priority in her life.
- The credit. She is masterful at this. While she is totally comfortable with accepting recognition for her good work, she is very quick to point out others who contributed to her success. She loves to share the spotlight with them.
- Your love and caring. KZ has never been one to play it safe. She does not live with the mentality that says, "I will give you my love

and support if you *first* show me *your* love and support." Most of us will not take the risk to give it first without knowing if it will be returned. I mean, what if I extend myself to you and then you take advantage of me, or laugh at me? No way. Most of us put up a thick, protective shield. We're all waiting for the other guy to make the first move. What if we all assumed, as KZ does, that the position of power belongs to the person who is willing to be vulnerable and extend their love. And if it's rejected, so be it.

3. Ask other people for their opinions and advice

I have heard it said that as human beings we strive for three things: looking good, being right and feeling important. When you ask others for the opinions and advice on certain matters, you give them the opportunity to experience all three. I'm not saying that you have to agree with what they say, I'm merely suggesting that you listen with interest and don't *dis*agree.

First of all, because you asked them, they believe that you think they are important and intelligent. Then, when you consider their ideas, they feel as though they are, perhaps, making a positive difference for you. And as they get to talk about a topic with which they are familiar, they get to look good.

KZ not only asks for my input, but she gives all my ideas careful consideration. There are times, of course, when she makes a different choice, and I totally respect her right to do so. And, when she does make a different choice, she doesn't apologize for her actions. She simply thanks me again for my assistance. And, I am extremely thankful that she does make up her own mind. I would not want to be responsible for suggesting a course of action that might backfire! I mean, if that happened, then I wouldn't get to look good or be right!

4. Write thank-you notes

I remember once, when I was feeling a little out of sorts, I received a thank-you card from KZ. The reason? There wasn't one. It was just to tell me that she thought that I was one of the most amazing women on the planet and that I was extremely important in her life. Another wow moment for me.

Let's do things like that for lots of people in our lives. Keep a box of note cards handy where you can see them and be reminded every day. Carry a few cards around with you so you can leave one behind when you need to. Write them to customers, bosses, co-workers, family members, friends. Don't allow yourself to rationalize not sending one with statements like, "Oh, I told him I appreciated it," or "I'm sure he knows how I feel," or "She's family, I don't need to send *her* a thank-you note." Do it anyway. It only takes a few minutes and it pays big dividends.

Now it is time to insert another warning: Remember to check out your intentions. If you are sending acknowledgment notes for the big dividends *you* will receive, it will ultimately backfire. If you do it, on the other hand, for the big dividends the other person will receive in the process, you will have served your purpose. The fact that in it there may be a benefit to you should always remain a distant second.

While the KZ Strategy alone would give you all the rapport and connection you would probably ever need with other people, I will add one more to the suggestion box. This one has worked extremely well in my life, also.

What's right today?

We know we talk to ourselves. But did you know that it is estimated that we have an average of about 40,000 thoughts per day? And get this, eighty to ninety percent of those thoughts are negative. If you doubt me, let's take a look at the beginning of a fairly typical day. See if any of the following internal dialogue sounds familiar to you.

"Is it 6:00 A.M. already? I don't want to get up."

"Gosh, my body aches."

"I shouldn't have eaten that second piece of pie."

"What's the matter with this stupid shower faucet?"

"I sure am dreading that meeting with the H.R. department this morning."

"Oh for heaven's sake. The dry cleaner didn't press this shirt right."

"Who ate the last bit of the cereal and didn't throw the empty box away?"

"Oh no. It's raining."

"Traffic is terrible."

"Again. Jones is late."

"Kramer needs to do something about his messy desk."

"This coffee tastes awful."

"Is he wearing *that* stupid tie again?"

And on and on and on.

Remember we talked about how we are continually asking ourselves questions? One question we ask, *a lot,* is "What's going to mess up today?" All the dialogue I just listed could be in direct response to that question. I asked bad quality questions and I got some bad quality answers.

We do this with people more than we might care to admit. I can always find what's wrong with those difficult individuals in my life because I'm looking for any and everything in their behavior which comes under the heading of, "What stupid thing is that idiot going to do next?" Ask and ye shall receive.

In order to build strong relationships I can use this strategy to my advantage. I can use it to find honest, legitimate things to acknowledge people for, and accordingly, it will help strengthen my relationships with those "difficult" people.

Enter George

If, from past experiences, I believe that George is a difficult person, when he walks by and smiles at me, my suspi-

cions lead me to the question, "What did he mean by that?"
I then will pull up some pretty interesting possibilities for
answers. None of which, by the way, may serve me. If
you, on the other hand, know George to be a wonderful,
open, honest fellow, when he smiles at you, you'll have a
totally different response.

Consider this. When you ask a question, it's as if you
enter a command on the keyboard of your computer brain.
You are, in effect, going through the following process:

Command: "Show me all the files under why
George, the jerk, smiled that ridiculous smile at
me."
Searching files . . .
Searching files . . .
Fifty-two matches found:

- Because he's an idiot . . .
- Because he's up to no good . . .
- Because he wants something from me .
- Because he's trying to impress me . . .
- Ad infinitum.

You see what happens? We only get a response to
the direct command we make. So, what would
happen if we asked a different question?

Command: "Could I be wrong about George?"
(Better question. Not as rich with possibility as
it could be but it's better.)
Searching files . . .
Searching files . . .
Searching files . . .
One match found:

- NO

Let's try another one.

Command: What positive qualities does George
possess which I haven't paid attention to in the
past?

Searching files . . .
Searching files . . .
Searching files . . .
No matches found

Go back again.

Command: Search more files under what *possible*
positive qualities George possesses that I
haven't paid attention to in the past?
Searching files . . .
Searching files . . .
Searching files . . .
Three matches found:

- He is always very punctual . . .
- His work is extremely thorough . . .
- He has a good laugh . . .

Well, there you have it. There actually are some positive qualities about George which you can now see because you found a way to access them. They were there all along, but because of the questions you were asking, you were unable to put your hands on them.

Just in terms of building stronger relationships, do you see how this could be a way to pull your focus in a different direction? And when you begin to see George as a man with positive qualities—and actually acknowledge him for them—you'll probably notice him starting to behave differently toward you.

So here's a suggestion. Post a large mat board on the wall with a heading that says, WHAT'S RIGHT TODAY? Ask people to find at least three right things that they notice other people doing during the day. Ask them then to jot down what they saw on a Post-it note and stick it on the board during the day.

Here's what happens. People start actually looking for what's right—and seeing lots more right things. Because they identify them and put them on the board, others get to feel acknowledged and appreciated for what they did. So not only will people be noticing more right things, they will start doing more right things.

By the way, in terms of motivating people and raising morale, this is a great idea. However, it won't continue to work forever. The secret to motivating people and keeping morale high is to employ many practices like this, lots of recognition, continuous acknowledgments, and reward systems and change them often. People begin to understand that they are valued, and they are important. They also become part of the solution.

To reiterate—everything in our lives that we aspire to achieve will be attained, to one degree or another, through the help of others. To paraphrase Zig Ziglar: in order to get more of what you want in life, help others get more of what they want. And, once again, by doing this, you are owning your power, utilizing it and sharing it generously. A win-win proposition.

Strategy No. 8

Communicate Wisely

Communication is the largest single factor determining what kinds of relationships a person makes with others and what happens to him or her in the world. It determines how we survive, how we develop intimacy, how productive we are, how we make sense and how we connect with our own divinity. —Virginia Satir

As much as we sometimes think that we can handle certain things by ourselves, the bottom line is that every single thing we do involves other people to one degree or another. And how do we get help or get what we need from others? We communicate that information in a variety of ways. Therefore, it stands to reason that the better quality communication we have, the greater influence we have, and thereby greater power to get what we need.

Everything communicates

We are never *not* communicating. If I walk into a room and say absolutely nothing—my silence speaks volumes. Whether I smile or I don't. Whether I lift one eyebrow or look away or shrug my shoulders. Everything communicates something. So let's break down our communication and see what the components are.

Most of us know that any message is made of three aspects: the verbal, the vocal and the visual. There are the words being used, the sound of the voice (rate, pitch, volume, and intonation), and visual cues of the sender (eye contact, gestures, facial expression, posture, positioning). Dr. Albert Mehrabian tells us that when there is any kind of an inconsistency between what we are saying and the way we are saying it, the breakdown of our message is approximately as follows:

Verbal—7 percent
Vocal—38 percent
Visual—55 percent

Are we being consistent with our messages? Are we being 100 percent truthful in our communication? Are we congruent? Congruency enhances credibility, which builds trust. Trust = power.

The meaning of the message

The meaning of any message lies squarely in what the receiver takes it to mean, regardless of the sender's intention. Accordingly, we need to take 100 percent responsibility for how our communication lands out in the world. The interesting thing is that usually, we don't really know how we are perceived out there. It becomes imperative, therefore, for us to hold a mirror up to ourselves and take an objective look.

A woman attending one of my seminars lamented the fact that other people were always accusing her of being angry, offensive and difficult to talk with. With a furrow in her brow and tight lips she snapped, "But they are so wrong! I am not angry! I don't know why they keep saying that!"

It was interesting. I tried to gently and lovingly hold up that mirror to her so that she could see what she was projecting and thereby understand why they might make that interpretation. She couldn't get it. She just kept saying, "But it isn't true! I'm a very happy, wonderful person!"

I asked, "Are they treating you as such?"

She responded, "No."

I then said, "OK, you are not getting the results that you want from other people. And in order to get those results, obviously something has to change. Now, as I see it, you have a two options. You can change what's happening on your face or you can wear a big sign around your neck that states in bold letters: 'I know my face looks angry and hostile, but it's not an accurate reflection of what I'm feeling—so just get over it'."

She indignantly replied, "Linda, I can't change my face."

"Ahhh but you can!" I responded. "I have done it myself."

I explained then how I had become aware of something that was happening on my face, which was undermining my credibility and preventing me from establishing rapport with others. It was during a time in my life when people seemed to be defensive with me a lot. Metaphorically, they didn't appear to want to play with me. I was a nice person. Why weren't people beating down my door to give me their business or invite me to their parties?

I remember one day I was preparing to leave for an appointment I had with the senior partners in a large law firm. I was going to tell them how my services as a communications consultant could benefit them. I was packing a few items on a counter in front of a large mirror and I was going over what I was going to say. I was looking down, packing, and talking out loud to myself. At one point while I was talking I looked up and saw my face in the mirror. I was chagrined.

The face I saw looking back at me was *not* at all consistent with what was going on in my head! I was excited and enthusiastic about what I was saying. My face, however, looked intense, stern and negative. I stopped dead in my tracks. In that moment I got it. This was why so many people seemed defensive with me. I was eliciting that response! I couldn't believe it.

The first thing I did was to start observing people who were easy to listen to, who were persuasive and positive. People I immediately liked, imbued with credibility and enjoyed being around. I noticed that there were no frowns.

In fact, if they weren't actually smiling, they were just short of it. They looked like a smile waiting to happen. Their eyes were open wide. Their eyebrows were lifted, not furrowed. Their face, in other words, was congruent with their message that what they were saying was exciting, interesting and worth considering.

I took the mental picture of that face, I went back to the mirror and tried to recreate it on myself. It was your basic joke. I looked like a cross between the cat that swallowed the canary and Gomer Pyle. But in the process of this silly experiment, I made a great discovery. Whenever I was thinking a thought that legitimately gave me a feeling a pleasure or joy, a look congruent with that feeling showed up on my face!

We can't manufacture a pleasant face. It comes from inside—from a pleasant thought, which gives rise to a positive feeling, which produces the appropriate look on our face. But then, once we know what it looks like, we can make the conscious choice to embody it more often. And, as I mention in the chapter on managing our emotions, sometimes if we merely change our physiology (our face), the emotions will follow.

Make no mistake. Powerful people are not those who throw their weight around and try to look as menacing as possible. Oh, they may get people to shrink back in fear and succumb to their every command. But this isn't *true power*. This is intimidation. This is oppressive, demeaning and self-damaging. It gives the perpetrator a *temporary* feeling of power, behind which lies anxiety, guilt and disease. We can make a different, more empowering choice, for ourselves and for others.

It will take a while for your new face to become an automatic, habitual behavior, but you will know it when it does. People start behaving differently to you. Your power base begins to widen as people are drawn to you, listen more openly to what you have to say and enjoy their interactions with you.

Listen for all you're worth

Dr. Phillip C. McGraw, in his fabulous book, *Life Strategies*, identifies ten characteristics which are common to all human beings. He says that incorporating them into your social interactions will change the course of your life. I mention the first five of these ten, because if we learn how to *really* listen to other people, we will be automatically honoring these five characteristics. In his words they are:

1. The number-one fear among all people is rejection.

2. The number-one need among all people is acceptance.

3. To manage people effectively, you must do it in a way that protects or enhances their self-esteem.

4. Everybody—and I mean everybody—approaches every situation with at least some concern about "what's in it for me?"

5. Everybody—and I mean everybody—prefers to talk about things that are important to them personally.

When we learn to listen well, in other words, to listen to understand, we are meeting the other person's need to be accepted. We tell them that they are important enough for us to give them our 100 percent attention and full interest. We are allowing them to talk about things that are important to them. We are establishing tremendous rapport.

Most people listen for the other person to shut up so that they can have the floor. And as such, every nonverbal indicator of the "listener" screams that information loudly. We fidget. Our eyes dart around. We sigh impatiently. And what does the other person usually do then? They either talk louder and more vehemently to make us understand or they give up, walk away, and write us off as uncaring, inattentive or, worse, a complete jerk.

If you want to validate someone as a worthwhile, important person, give them your *active* listening, the kind of listening that takes energy and attention. Aspects of good listening include:

- Give feedback and paraphrase content
- Give feedback and paraphrase feeling ("Sounds like you were upset.")
- Clarify for meaning ("Let me make sure I understand you—").
- Maintain good eye contact.
- Eliminate distractions to the best of your ability. (Close door, hold all calls, move items from directly in front of you.)

Avoid:

- Telling your own story ("The same thing happened to me!")
- Giving advice ("Here's what you should do—")
- Trying to minimize their feelings ("Oh, I'm sure it wasn't all that bad.")

When you give this kind of listening to those around you, you are building rapport and strengthening your relationships.

Listen up!

Tonight—or even right now—put this book down and go actively listen, in the manner described above, to another person. First of all, notice how difficult it is. Many of us feel as if we can't exist on the planet if we're not telling other people what they should do in order to make their lives better.

The second thing I ask you to notice is what happens to the other person when you are doing your job. Notice how validated they seem to feel. You will begin to hear them say with enthusiasm, things like, "that's exactly right!" and "yes, absolutely!" I assure you, they will walk away feeling like you totally understand. And, on some level, they believe you must be a very smart, astute individual if you find their stuff as interesting and important as they do.

I can unequivocally state this: the reason I managed to escape from my captor on that cold December day was directly attributable to this strategy. I knew, beyond a doubt, that my only hope for escape was if I could establish enough rapport with him that he would let his guard down.

I listened for all I was worth. I listened to him tell me about what a miserable life he had and how other people were idiots and could never be trusted. I listened intently as he told me about how he had to get other people before they got him first. And as I listened, I realized this was no time to be offering such inane comments as, "Oh, now I'm sure you don't really feel that way," or "Well, now have you ever considered trying to do *this* the next time that happens?" or "Oh my gosh, the same thing happened to me—let me tell you all about it."

I know this sounds ludicrous, but is it any smarter to respond like that to a friend or a loved one or a co-worker? Let's make a new choice. Begin to practice your good listening skills as soon as possible.

Getting clear

Have you ever made a request or a comment and noticed that the other person seemed to have an inappropriate response to it? Didn't you wonder exactly what their problem was? You thought you were crystal clear on what you meant, and as far as you were concerned, any reasonable person would have understood your meaning. So what happened?

Ahhh. Just because something lives very vividly in our minds, that doesn't mean the other person gets it. And herein lies the challenge. How do I make certain that what I am intending to say is what's being heard? Also, how do I know that what I am hearing the other person say is what they are intending for me to hear?

Let's start with an example. We all want to feel love. And in a love relationship, we want to believe that our partner loves us. But how do we know that they do? Is it in something they say or do? What information do I pick up that tells me, "Yes, I know I am loved."

I recently asked my husband, "What has to happen in order for you to feel loved?" He looked back at me and said, "Excuse me?"

I said, "Well, you *know* I love you, but *how* do you know that? What exactly tells you that you are loved?"

He thought for a moment and finally he said, "I don't know. It's just a feeling."

I remarked, "Isn't this curious? In order for me to give you more of whatever it is that makes you feel loved, I need to know what that is—but you can't tell me. It has to come in through your senses, doesn't it? Is it something I say? Something I do? A way I look at you? A way that I touch you? What?"

He said, "Oh, yeah. It's that smile and that look in your eye. It's the way you tell me how you appreciate what I do for you."

Bingo! We just made an important discovery. I now have information that I can use consciously. I thought that if I gave him cards and little presents for no reason, if I always looked my very best when we went out together, and I told him daily how much I loved and cherished him, then he would feel loved. And why did I think these things let him know that I loved him? Because those are some of the things that let me know that *I* am loved.

Well, isn't this curious? I communicate my love in a way that works for me and is compatible with my needs and he communicates his love in a way that works for him and is compatible with his needs. He could care less about mushy cards and funny presents. He needs smiles and looks and verbal appreciation for his good deeds. Now that I am aware, I can communicate accordingly.

There are certain feelings that you are trying to evoke in other people. Feelings of love, trust, respect, etc. Do you know what they need from you in order to experience those feelings? It may not be what you think it is.

Do you know what your teenager needs in order to feel comfortable bringing his friends over to the house?

Do you know what your friend needs in order to have what he or she considers a good friendship?

I just this moment stopped my writing, called my friend Kathy and I asked her, "Kathy, for you, what is the most important thing in a friendship?" She responded without hesitation, "Loyalty." I then asked, "What has to happen in order for you to know that loyalty is present in your friendship?" She thought a moment and replied, "Well, it's when you can say what you feel, or express your fears knowing that the other person will love you anyway and will remain your friend. It's where you can be honest."

Great information to know.

Action idea

List at least six people who are important to you and ask them the kinds of questions I just laid out in the above examples. See what responses you get. Talk about what you need also. Communicate openly, clearly and congruently. Listen attentively, actively and effectively. Watch your circle of influence grow and expand.

Notice how your relationships become stronger and more meaningful for everyone involved.

Strategy No. 9

Master Your Emotions

Anybody can become angry—that is easy. But to be angry with the right person, to the right degree, at the right time, for the right reason, and in the right way—that is not easy.—Aristotle

Have you ever paid a price for not being able to manage your emotions? Maybe a relationship was damaged, or a business deal was stopped short. I know it has happened to me in the past. During the times when I allowed myself to be totally reactive to someone else's negative attitude, I discovered that all I really did was exacerbate the problem.

I remember a time specifically, early one morning, when I was setting up a conference room for a meeting. I expected about 100 people and the room was not at all set to my specifications. Try as I may, I couldn't find any hotel staff to correct the problem. Everyone said that it was someone else's job—but there seemed to be no "someone else" to be found. Finally, an extremely upset man walked in. It turns out he was a worker in the restaurant who had been summoned by another staff member to come help me. It was crystal clear. He did not want to be there.

I decided the moment he walked in that I would *not* let his mood impact my communication. I smiled, I apologized and asked if he would be so kind as to help me move several tables. As he stomped over and grabbed a table, his curt, angry response was, "This is *not* my job." I replied, "Oh, I know—and I am so grateful you agreed to help."

"Yeah, well," he went on, "I have a *million* other things to do. I don't have time to be doing *this*."

I took a deep breath. Once again I remarked—fairly calmly, "I know it must be frustrating for you. Oh, we need to put those tables over here."

He shot a stinging look at me. "No, *ma'am. We* don't need to put those tables over here. *We* need to be in the kitchen doing what *we* are supposed to be doing. This is *not* my job!"

My teeth are now starting to grind. My eyes are getting more narrow. My nostrils are beginning to flare. Through clenched teeth I comment, "Yes. I *know* this is not your job."

"You're damned right it's not my job!" he shouts back angrily.

It was at this point that my eyes crossed and the smoke came out of my ears. I had my hands on the edge of a table, which I grabbed by the corners, lifted about a foot off the ground and promptly slammed back down on the floor in perfect timing with my loud, angry *"I know it's not your job! You have told me that ten times already!"*

I realized at this point that I had just given this man exactly what he wanted. He threw down the table he was moving, looked me squarely in the face and said, "I don't need this @!*!" He then turned on his heel and walked out of the room.

Whereas before I at least had *some* help (grumpy though he may have been), I now had none. I was then left to move all the tables by myself. Guess I showed him, huh?

You can probably recall a similar incident or two when losing your cool has cost you, as well.

But what about this? Have you ever had a situation where just the opposite happened? It seemed like everything around you was falling apart and you were like a rock. You saved the day. Other people were flipping out and you held it together, solved the problem and emerged as the hero.

This, too, has happened to me. As a matter of fact, I am now aware that it was my ability to manage my emotions on the day I was kidnapped that kept me safe. Remember I said there was a Linda look-alike running around in my head screaming and yelling hysterically? Well, it was my ability to keep her under control that saved my life.

So how did we do it? Why did we lose it in one situation and hold it together in another one? What determines our emotional state at any given moment?

Thus far, I have been able to come up with three possibilities. One is drugs. Certainly drugs can impact our emotions. So let's rule that one out right now as an option. Two is our focus—where we put our attention—either internally (thoughts) or externally (out in the world). Three is our physiology—our bodies, movement.

I used to think that my emotions just sort of dropped in on me out of nowhere. I would hear myself say things like, "Oh, I don't know, I'm just feeling a little sad today." Or happy or pensive or depressed or whatever. I didn't realize that this is not the way it works. Most of the time, my emotions are a direct result of my thoughts, or what I am doing with my body.

Let's look first at my thoughts in the example with my hotel room challenge. I was doing pretty well at first. I was focused on the fact that I had some help—any help. Where I blew it was when I started focusing on his comments. So what could I have done instead? I could have continued to say something such as, "I understand" and then immediately turn my attention to other matters such as where I needed to put my overhead screen, or did I have enough transparencies. I could have started thinking about the great turnout I was expecting. I could have (and this is not as strange as it sounds) reached over, grabbed my cassette player, thrown the headphones on and gone about my work. I guarantee you, when I turn my attention (my focus) to great, funky, dance music, I do not care what goes on with the rest of the world, I start feeling fabulous! If I had done that, I would have ended up getting what I needed—and feeling great. That would be using my power consciously and constructively to manage my own emotions.

Shake it, baby!

In terms of our physiology and how that can impact our emotions, I turn once again to music and dancing. Have you ever found yourself at the end of a long day where you feel tired, sluggish and emotionally spent? You just want to plop in a chair and feel sorry for yourself. Then, you turn on the radio, or put on a CD and *that* tune starts playing. You know the one. The one where you feel like Michael or Janet Jackson when you dance to it. So, what the heck, no one's around. You get up and start dancing.

Whoa! Get back! You are movin' with the groove! You are the hottest thing to hit the dance floor since the artist formerly known as Prince. With wild abandon you come up with moves that even astound you!

And then the song is over. You glance over at the mirror. Your face is flushed. There is a huge smile grinning back at you. All of a sudden you notice that you're not tired anymore! In fact, you feel great!

Cool. You took action. You moved your body. You felt better. Don't you love it when that happens? Then do it more often! Like Joan Baez once said, "Action is the antidote to despair."

The success cycle

Here's how this works:

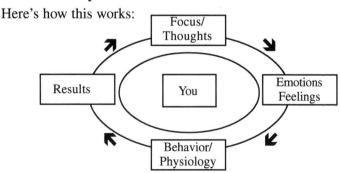

Notice how the arrows flow from the thoughts to the emotions. The emotions then impact our behaviors and from those behaviors we get certain results in the world. We then look at the results we got, formulate certain thoughts and we are back in the cycle again.

Here's an outstanding example of one man who was able to manage his emotions brilliantly with this model and create extremely positive outcomes.

I was picking up my rental car at an airport one day. The shuttle bus dropped me off at the lot, I selected a car from the Emerald Isle and proceeded to the kiosk to check out. I noticed that when I drove up, the man in the booth had his back to me. Now it's important to mention at this point that I was not particularly happy nor sad, I was simply in a nice, neutral place. When I stopped he turned to greet me and here's what I saw.

First of all, he looked thrilled to see me. He had this huge smile on his face, like I was his long-lost best friend. His enthusiasm was infectious as he said, "Hi! It's great to see you! How *are* you?"

I could not contain my automatic response. I chuckled—out loud. I said, "Well, I'm good, how are you?" He responded back with that same outstanding smile, "I am absolutely great!" Once again, I laughed. And by now, I am quite curious.

"Young man," I said, "May I ask you, why are you so absolutely great?"

"Well, because I have such fabulous customers! They are just like you, they are always laughing and smiling!"

It didn't take me long to figure this one out. I immediately said, "Oh, young man, may I suggest that happy, smiling customers are not just *showing up* for you? You are *creating* them!" To which he responded, "Well, I don't know how they got here, I'm just glad they came!" And he laughed again.

I drove away thinking, "Oh my gosh. This is that cycle for managing your emotions." Think about it. He walks into his little booth in the morning and maybe he's not particularly sad or happy, but he starts thinking things like, "I love my job. I have the greatest customers. They are so wonderful, they're always laughing and smiling. Seems like they come in droves, too. And, oh boy, they're going to be coming soon!" Notice at this point he starts to get resultant emotions from his thoughts. He's excited, happy, expectant.

We then drive up, he turns and takes one look and says with joy and glee, "You're here! Hooray!" (behaviors). We look back and can't help but smile and say hi, (results) at which point he says to himself, "See! I *do* have great customers!" (back to the thoughts again). What a fabulous, productive cycle.

Now we could have had just the opposite happen. What if we had another man go to work in the morning with a different mindset. Maybe he walks in and his first thought is, "What a miserable place to work! I'm in a damned *phone booth*, for crying out loud. And not only that, I have to contend with all those stupid, crabby, impatient customers."

Those thoughts lead to predictable feelings of anger, resentment, misery. Then, we show up, he turns and looks at us and snaps, "Well?" We look back and say curtly, "Well, hello to you, too." At which point he thinks to himself, "Yep. Like I said, crabby, cranky, impatient customers. What a miserable job."

Ah, but once again, this man, too, was creating the people around him.

So here's the question. What kind of people are you creating in your life? Are you surrounded by happy, smiling, friendly people? Then take some credit for that. Or, are you surrounded by angry, negative, miserable people? You might have something to do with that, also.

It's about attitude, isn't it? And, as I said before, attitude isn't something we get *from* life, it's something we bring *to* life. If we are going to wander around waiting for other people to do something *first* to make us feel good, then we are once again, giving our power away. It reminds me of an old Chinese proverb: "He who waits for a roast duck to fly into his mouth must wait a very, very long time."

Do you want happiness in your life? Then be happy. And how do we get happy? Focus on the things which make us happy.

Make a gratitude list

On a sheet of paper (or two) make a long list of all the things in your life that you have to be grateful for. Include every person, every joy and every challenge which made you a stronger, better person. Include your dog, your cat, your education, your favorite teacher, your eyesight, your feet, your nice-looking ears. Go crazy. Have a ball. I promise you this, you will change your emotional state by just writing these things down. Then put this list where you can get your hands on it and read it every day. Add things to it as you think of them. You cannot feel anger and gratitude at the same time. You can't feel sorry for yourself and grateful simultaneously. It's a powerful use of the focus principle.

How may I serve you?

I believe it was Albert Einstein who wrote that, "Only a life lived for others is a life worth living."

The bottom line on this is *give*. Give your time, your energy, your resources, your love. Share freely. Open your heart. Allow every fear of being taken advantage of disappear from your consciousness. All the goodness that you give out will return back to you. Don't look for it to come back. Don't ask for it to be returned. Just give your gifts.

When you give those gifts to others, there are much, much greater gifts that you are giving yourself in the process. You are giving yourself the peace of mind that you are living by powerful principles. You are giving yourself joy in knowing that you are making a positive difference in people's lives. You are giving yourself the same love that you are extending out to the world. Once again, you are a part of the whole. What you impress upon the whole impacts you as well.

Change your internal conversation

One reason we are in such a cranky mood so much of the time is because of our daily copious negative thoughts. Remember? Appxomiately 40,000 thoughts—eighty to ninety percent of which are negative. We are focused on things that create crankiness. Some of the thoughts are about ourselves—and many are about all those other idiots out there who don't behave.

It's time to stop this self-defeating habit.

Have you ever talked yourself out of a good idea? It goes something like this: You had an idea. At first, you thought, "Wow! That's great!" Then, the more you thought about it, the more reasons you came up with why it would never work. And, of course, you never even tried because, well, what would be the point? It would never work.

Have you ever made some simple error and then pro-ceeded to call yourself names? Things such as, "I am such a jerk! I can't believe I was so stupid?" Sound familiar?

Please, please take very seriously the words of Dr. Joyce Brothers who said, "You cannot consistently per-form in a manner inconsistent with how you see yourself." And I would add, or how you are talking to yourself, which of course, comes directly out of how you see yourself.

So, if you want to have more empowering, produc-tive emotions and feelings, then change what you are tell-ing yourself.

Pick powerful words

Here's Mark Twain again: " A powerful agent is the right word. Whenever we come upon one of these intensely right words . . . the resulting effect is physical as well as spiri-tual, and electrically prompt."

Our words, just like the pictures we create in our mind, have a strong impact on our minds and bodies—and out in the world, as well.

And remember what we discussed earlier—the conscious mind does the talking and defining, and the subconscious mind simply says, "OK, we'll make it happen." Again, it is not the function of your subconscious mind to try and talk you out of anything, to rationalize or reason with you. It merely complies with the orders and does whatever it has to do to make it happen.

And here's what we are up against. Did you know that in the English language, we have more than 500,000 words? And linguists suggest that the average person has a working vocabulary of only between 2,000 and 10,000. That's amazing to me! But here's something even more amazing. I found one source that suggests there are more than 3,000 words that relate to human emotions. Of those 3,000 words the ratio of negative emotions to positive emotions was almost two to one, or said another way, I have twice as many words at my disposal to tell you how crummy I feel, or how miserable the world is, as I do positive ones to express my joy and happiness.

Let's take a look at the words we choose when we speak. For instance, when you go to a movie, do you want to see one that is "nice" or one that is "fabulous?" Do you want get a new outfit that is "adequate" or one that is "spectacular?" Do you prefer to feel "OK" or "ecstatic?" Would you like to be "all right" or "outrageously wonderful?" As you consciously choose your words, you'll notice that they begin to operate on that physical level that Twain was referring to. We don't create our words—they are creating us!

Let's look on the other side of the coin. Would you prefer to be "overwhelmed," or "momentarily on pause." When something goes wrong do you choose to be "devastated" or "taken aback"? Would you like to define yourself as "computer idiot" or "an open, eager willing student?"

And if someone comes up to you and asks you how you are doing, how do you normally respond? Your response, once again, is creating your reality.

I have a friend whom I have known for a long, long time. She is an outstandingly talented, beautiful, loving, woman, although I don't believe that is how *she* holds herself. Her experience in life says that she thinks something different. I can tell you exactly how she would answer the question, "How are you?" if I called her right now. She would say, with a sigh, "Well, I'm surviving."

Is that the most I can hope or aim for? To merely be surviving?

Have you ever said, "I am just exhausted. I am overwhelmed. I am going crazy." Don't do that!

Dr. Norman Cousins, author of *The Anatomy of an Illness* said, "Words can kill." He said that when a patient was diagnosed and had an actual word to define his symptoms, he got sicker. Words like, "cancer," "Parkinsons's disease" and "heart disease" tended to induce extreme fear and panic in patients. Those feelings (which were probably preceded by some pretty graphic mental pictures) then began to undermine their body's immune systems.

In a study conducted by John A. Bargh, a psychologist at New York University and a leading investigator of what he calls "the automaticity [sic] of being," college students first completed a language test that, for some of them contained words related to a stereotype of the elderly. These were words such as "Florida," "sentimental," and "wrinkle." Immediately afterward, those exposed to these stereotypical words walked much more slowly down an adjoining hallway as they departed, apparently responding to the automatically evoked notion of physical deterioration among seniors. Interestingly, they also remembered fewer features of the experimental room when questioned later.

So, which would you rather be, "dead tired," or a "little less than zippy?"

The choice is up to you.

Develop your own mantra

If we're talking to ourselves anyway, and we know that our words are having an immediate impact on our emotions, then why don't we develop specific phrases or mantras to use when the tension is high and emotions could run hot.

I did exactly this. I had once noticed than whenever my friend, Janice, would start to get reactive in a situation over which she had no control, she would start saying to herself something such as, "Let it go, breathe it out, move it on. Let it go, breathe it out, move it on." And she would repeat it over and over until she felt herself calm down.

I loved this mantra, so I borrowed it, and used it whenever I needed it. I know that my husband had heard me muttering the phrase to myself at various times although I wasn't sure he knew exactly what I was saying.

I remember one day, after I had been on the phone trying to get through the most convoluted voice mail system in the world, I began to get frustrated. John was busy doing something in the background and after twenty-five minutes I was still on the phone, getting the run around, being put on hold, having to explain the same problem six different times only to finally come back to the original person who didn't know what in the heck I was talking about.

I hung up the phone and started snorting and complaining about the poor service I had gotten when finally, John looked up at me from his project and said, "Honey, do that thing. . . .You know, that thing . . . that . . . 'Roll it over, kick it out, cough it up!'"

First of all, the image he created immediately changed my emotional state. I went from feeling cranky to feeling silly in a heartbeat. He reminded me how quickly our focus can shift our emotions. Secondly, he reconnected me with the idea of having a quick mantra ready to use. Obviously, your mantra can be whatever works for you.

So, flip it over, spread it out, burp it up. Do whatever it takes to get the frustration out of you so that you remain at the helm. You stay in control of your emotions. You achieve your desired outcomes.

Strategy No. 10

Practice Lifelong Learning

To build power, even to keep that which you have now, you must take personal responsibility for your continued learning.
—Price Pritchett, author of *Mindshift*

In order to remain in a place of power in the world, we must be fully equipped with information. It has been said that the future belongs to the competent. I would add, and so does the present. And how do we become competent? We learn more. We begin to embrace what the Japanese call *kaizen*, the commitment to constant and never ending improvement.

We live in an age where we are being bombarded with new information. In the year 1500 A.D. it took 250 years for information to double. Today it takes less than eighteen months! The National Research Council says that it used to take seven to fourteen years for half of a worker's skills to become obsolete. Today it takes only three to five years for fifty percent of our skills to become obsolete.

I am painfully aware of this. I bought a Palm Pilot—a small hand-held computer—not too long ago, and was really excited about using it as I traveled about. I kept thinking that as soon as I got a few extra minutes I would figure out how to use it. Those few minutes never showed up and now there are several newer models available that make mine look archaic!

Here's our challenge. With so much information bombarding us every day, how do we gain access to what we need and assimilate it more easily. I know that frequently I feel like I am in the pounding surf, and just when I think I've gotten a bit of information that will propel me forward, I get knocked over by another crashing wave of information. I know I'll never, ever get it all—but I'd much rather ride the crest of the waves instead of being beaten up down below.

The great news is that learning has never been easier. It used to be that we had to either go to a library or go back to school. Not so today. We can access information in a variety of ways. You can tap into the Internet or check out the learning channels on your television. There are seminars and workshops offered every day in thousands of cities across our country.

It has been reported that both Harry Truman and Earl Nightingale read every book in their respective hometown libraries. When the vice presidents of Federal Express were asked why they thought that founder, Fred Smith, had been so successful with the company, their responses, across the board, were that he was "an avid reader." Many leading authorities including Brian Tracy and Dr. Stephen Covey suggest that we read at least one hour per day.

When I heard this, my first thought was, "I don't have an extra hour per day! Where can I possibly extract another hour out of the day?"

I heard it once said that successful people utilize time that unsuccessful people waste. Look around. Where are you wasting time? AAA reports that we spend an average of 500 to 1,000 hours per year in our car and that number will likely increase. In fact, some futurists predict that while traffic jams consumed an estimated 1.6 billion lost work hours in 1989, they will consume 8.1 billion work hours in 2005.

We could get our doctoral degrees in our car if we could just figure out a way to get it accredited. Turn your automobile into a learning machine. Invest in audiocassette (or CD) programs on a variety of topics.

Where does the time go?

Speaking of wasting time, I read an article in a recent edition of *USA Today* that defined how we spend the hours in our day. The author quoted from a variety of researchers cited in *Faster: The Acceleration of Just About Everything*, by James Gleick. It looked like this:

- Seven hours and eighteen minutes asleep, a twenty percent drop from a century ago
- Six hours working, if we're employed
- Four hours doing housework, if we're women, less than half of that if we're men
- Three hours watching TV, double the 1965 figure
- One hour and twenty-six minutes on line, if we're on-line computer users
- One hour eating
- Fifty-two minutes on the phone
- Forty-one minutes reading magazines and newspapers
- Thirty-one minutes caring for children
- Twenty-nine minutes visiting other people
- Sixteen minutes reading books
- Seven minutes caring for pets and plants
- Four minutes having sex—the same amount the government says we spend filling out government forms

Isn't that interesting? A couple things jump out at me when I look at those figures. First of all, *three hours watching TV*? Good heavens! While we don't spend three hours in front of the television in my home, I do know that there are times when my television set sometimes seems to wield more power than I do. Isn't it easy to get lost in the Bermuda Triangle of Television? But while I'm lulled into a state of zombiosity watching Vanna saunter back and forth turning over letters, I am simultaneously throwing away precious, irretrievable, life enhancing minutes. Let's refuse to do that any longer. You can easily capture an extra hour by turning off the TV.

Oh, and about that four minutes we devote to having sex—never mind.

One thing you can do to keep your learning curve high is to keep a cassette player on counters throughout your house. Then, when you are doing some mindless chore, such as folding laundry, cooking or washing dishes, have something playing in the background. A portable cassette player with headphones is excellent to use when you are working out, walking the dog, vacuuming or mowing the lawn.

Don't wear your headphones during those last precious four minutes, however.

Also, remember this. Research tells us that we have to revisit material as much as seven times before we actually retain the information. Have you ever read a great book and, when you finished it, remember thinking, "Wow! This is the greatest! This will really change everything for me!" Did you then notice that after three or four weeks nothing in your life had actually altered? What happened?

You never went back to the book to reinforce the information. Those great ideas fell through the trapdoor of your brain. How do you prevent this from happening? Here are some great ideas.

1. Reread or listen again to the information.
2. Take notes (if listening to audio).
3. Highlight ideas (in books).
4. Teach someone else what you learn.
5. At each reading or listening session, pick one idea to practice. Then immediately implement it. Practice until you get it.
6. Reread your notes occasionally or scan the book for the highlighted areas.

Now that we found a few ways to find that hour per day for reading and expanding our minds, how do we then combat the old, but-I-don't-have-the-money argument? Quite simply, I say, get over it. Do what you have to do (legally, morally and ethically, of course). To earn more, we MUST learn more!

Going back to 1994. I'm suddenly alone. I have no real income. I have absolutely no savings. I have been given one year's modest "severance pay," my little house and my car. My tendency at this point was to hoard. To scratch. To get some meager little job and live out the rest of my life humbly, counting pennies and clipping coupons (not that clipping coupons is such a bad idea). I thank God that I chose another path.

I wanted to be a professional speaker. I wanted to write. I wanted to positively impact people's lives and give them not only the hope that they, too, could rise above their conditions and challenges and achieve their dreams and goals, but the skills and tools they needed to help them do it.

I knew what I had to do in order to extricate myself from the powerlessness I was experiencing and would continue to experience if I stayed where I was. I had to take some major risks and get way outside my comfort zone.

I looked at my educational level. It wasn't bad, but by itself it wasn't going to take me where I wanted to go. I had an undergraduate degree in social work and a master of fine arts degree in professional actor training. So if I wanted to be a professional actor (as I was for many years), fine, but even for that I wouldn't get cast for a role because I had a degree. I would get cast if I was good enough and was exactly what they were looking for.

What I learned from my life as a actor was that the entertainment industry went beyond competitive to insane. There was way too much left up to chance, like whether or not you may happen to remind the casting director of his ex-sister-in-law whom he detested. One of my professors in graduate school once commented, "Linda, I don't think you have the killer instinct that you will need in order to make it in this business. You've got to be willing to step over dead bodies." Now isn't that an attractive image? Well, he nailed it. It wasn't going to be my life path.

So my formal education wasn't sufficient in and of itself. I knew I needed more education. I needed the tools to help me build the life I desired. I needed an overall plan.

So, here was my "business plan," if you will. My first task was to sell my car. Now, I have to tell you, this was a pretty nifty car. It was a gorgeous white BMW 325I convertible. I *loved* driving this car. I did not want to let it go. It was zippy and beautiful and paid for. But, as such, I began to view it as a highly valuable asset. I also began to see it as representative of a life in which any good I received came from someone else. I knew that I did not want that reminder. If I was going to have a great car, I wanted to buy it myself. Oh what pride and passion and power I would feel, I thought, when I could purchase whatever car I wanted with money I earned. That picture was extremely compelling and motivating to me.

I sold the car, bought a perfectly wonderful used car and walked away with $10,000 in my pocket. I now had capital with which to invest in myself. I soon learned that $10,000 was not quite as princely a sum as it first appeared. Nevertheless, it got me started.

I joined a health club and began to work out regularly. I learned to love my time at the gym. I was investing in my good health and the results were extremely positive.

I spent a goodly amount (OK, a *massive* amount) of money on Anthony Robbins' yearlong program for Life Mastery encompassing focus on finances, relationships, health and career. During the year, the workshops took place in Maui, Palm Springs, Chicago and Phoenix, and the tuition did not pay for travel, hotels and food. It became a huge investment. Now, looking back, I can say unequivocally that what I got out of that experience was worth 100 times what I paid for it.

I attended other workshops and seminars. I bought books, audiotapes and more books. I listened to some of the same things over and over again. Sometimes I would find myself saying things I didn't know I knew. The information was actually beginning to sink in!

I wasn't exactly out of the woods, however. I was totally out of reserve cash and had actually started relying on credit cards to take care of necessities and support myself. I had to hire a production company to create a demo video of me showcasing my skill as a speaker. It, of course, ended up costing twice what I had originally projected. I was going into debt fast.

There were times when my faith waned drastically. I felt alone and sometimes afraid. But here's what was so great. When those times occurred, there was always a tape or a resource to help me get through them!

I remember once when I found myself feeling particularly fearful, I did what I frequently did. I went to my local bookstore and browsed through the self-help section to see who would be available to help me right then. That day, I remember picking up Dr. Susan Jeffers' wonderful book, *Feel the Fear and Do It Anyway*. It was as if she was speaking directly to me. I remember reading her following words: "If everybody feels fear when approaching something totally new in life, yet so many are out there 'doing it' despite the fear, then we must conclude that *fear is not the problem.*"

In that moment I realized what she was telling us. It is not the fear itself that keeps me locked down. It is how I hold the fear. Obviously, the other person, who also experiences the same fear but moves forward anyway, simply has a different perspective on that fear. They do not let it paralyze them and become "the reason" they refrain from taking action. They just acknowledge the fear and blast on through.

So, it was back to the drawing board. I kept on track with my quest to get work as a speaker and trainer. I felt I was fairly well prepared so I continued to mail out promotional packets. And ultimately one of the tapes paid off. I was invited to fly out to Kansas City to do a live audition for a position as a free-lance trainer with SkillPath Seminars.

And speaking of fear—even with more than twenty years experience behind me as a professional actress (I had performed on the legitimate stage, in feature films and television programs and in dozens of regional and national television commercials), even with all that, the experience was nerve-racking. I just kept repeating over and over to myself, "You are prepared. You know what you are doing. You are good. Now, feel the fear and do it anyway." Within a few minutes after my audition, they offered me the position.

I am clear that this opportunity presented itself to me because:

> a. I decided what I wanted (what)
> b. I created a picture of what it would look like if I didn't get it (why)
> c. I invested in myself in order to learn more and be prepared (how)
> d. When I felt the predictable, ensuing fear, I did not let it stop me.

Take care of the whole goose

OK, so now I realize the importance of ongoing learning—of being prepared and ready to avail oneself of opportunities when they are presented. But as with every good awareness there's a cautionary aspect. In this case, it's the potential burnout.

When I first started on my "quest for more knowledge," I was somewhat maniacal. I constantly had my face in a book or headphones on. What I began to realize was that the quest for never ending improvement included taking care of other aspects besides my intellect and my physical self. I had been neglecting the improvement of my spiritual and my social self. I began to realize that I needed quiet, meditative, reflective time to renew and refresh my spirit. I also began to understand the need to simply be with friends, for no other reason than just to connect.

All these aspects can be found in the seventh habit of the *7 Habits of Highly Effective People*. This habit is referred to as "Sharpen the Saw."

The metaphor is that one cannot expect to effectively saw a pile of wood with a saw that is dull and in ill repair. The saw is the tool. The better shape the tool is in, the more effective you are at accomplishing your task. Accordingly a person cannot expect to effectively manage the challenges of life if they allow themselves (the saw) to become overused, burned out and spent.

I invite you to consider this awareness as you prepare to kick this strategy into gear. Take care of all four of the following aspects of your life—physical, mental, social and spiritual—so that you are in good health. The entire system has to be in good working order in order to function effectively.

And in terms of the power inherent in ongoing learning, I once heard it said that no matter what you want to do in your life, if someone else has mastered it, then study what they have done. Their experience can become a road map to help you get where you want to go and to alert you to possible pitfalls on the highway ahead.

You know what you want. You have a map to help you get there. You now have the power to create what you want in your life.

Conclusion

I'm freezing. I can feel myself shivering from somewhere deep within my being. It's been five hours since this nightmare began and, in spite of the Valium I swallowed a few hours ago, I am more alert than ever. I am now dressed in a bathrobe, which he allowed me to put on after the rape.

Well, I think it was rape. I'm not sure. Maybe it really wasn't. I certainly didn't put up a fight. Isn't rape when you scream and try to fight off your attacker? I think it is. He said, "Here's what's going to happen," and I said, "OK." No, I guess that's not rape. Of course, he *did* have a gun.

I'm confused. I'm too cold. I have to get back to the task at hand.

He's had so much of that whiskey to drink he's beginning to lose some of his edge. This is good. He's getting a little sloppy.

We are sitting on the sofa. He's holding the gun in his lap pointed out away from him. I'm so thirsty. Maybe he'll let me go into the kitchen and get some water.

"Can I go get some water for us?" I ask.

"Sure. Get some water."

I stand and move in front of him to walk around to the kitchen. When I am directly in front of him, I hear the gun go off. It sounds like an explosion. It is deafening. "Oh my God," I think to myself. "He just shot me! Well, this is it. This is how it ends."

I'm frozen to the spot. The terror overtakes me and I choke. I desperately look to see where the bullet hit me. I don't feel anything yet, but I guess that's what happens when you are shot. You are too stunned to know what's going on.

I don't see any blood. My eyes quickly dart to him. He's looking at the gun, incredulously.

"How did that happen?" he asks with this mystified look on his face.

"Didn't you just fire the gun at me?"

"Well, I guess it went off of its own accord. It's got this hair trigger and man, is it touchy."

My heart is pounding in my ears. My body is shaking. I can hardly speak. Keep it together, Linda. Keep it together.

Finally, I croak. "Well, wouldn't it be awful if after all this you *accidentally* shot me?" I'm wondering who is speaking for me, saying these clever things.

He laughs wryly. I am about to gag.

"I'll get some water, OK?

"Sure," he replies.

I go into the kitchen. My pulse is racing. My eyes are scanning every inch of the back door leading out to where the car is parked. He had forced me to drive us here in the car he stole from the law office and I remember carefully leaving the keys in the ignition before he pulled me out of the car. God. It is so close. How do I get to the car?

I notice that there is a bolt lock on the back door. The door leads to a screened porch with another bolted lock. About fifteen feet away from the screen door sits the waiting car. Oh, but look. The car is facing the wrong way.

This house he directed me to is the only house on a small cul-de-sac at the end of a very long dirt road in a heavily wooded area. The car is now pointed toward the trees, not back toward the main road. When I make my escape, will I have enough time to get the car turned around? Never mind. Cross that bridge when you get to it.

When I open the refrigerator I see some hamburger meat thawed on a plate. My mind is working so incredibly fast that somehow, I am beginning to see a pattern. A possible scenario is playing out at warp speed on the chessboard in my mind.

I walk back into the living room and ask him if he would like me to make him a hamburger. He says yes and gets up to go to the bathroom. His back is to me as he walks down the short hall. In a heartbeat I turn, rush to the back door and throw the bolt. The damned thing sounds like a cannon! I cough loudly to cover the sound of the bolt. I somehow even structured the sound of my cough to be on a similar pitch as the bolt noise.

I rush back to the living room. He's still in the bathroom. I can hear him urinating. My heart is pounding.

"Do you want mustard or ketchup?" I shout.

"Mustard," he replies.

I rush back to the door, throw it open, cross the porch, unlock the screen, grab the handle and push. Oh my God, the door won't open. It's stuck. I push again with my whole body. The door gives way with a screech. He must have heard that. I fly over to the car and jump in.

By now I can hear him behind me. I fire up the car and slam it into reverse. I back up, go forward, back up, go forward, back up and now I'm heading down the dirt road. I can hear shots being fired. Are they coming in through the back window? I'm not sure.

I'm driving at a speed much too fast for this road. My car is fishtailing back and forth. Dirt is flying up obscuring my vision. The trees are too close. I'm probably going to hit one. My foot on the accelerator is shaking so wildly, I can barely control it. It seems like forever before the main road appears, and when it does, I take a hard left turn onto it, with no regard whatsoever for oncoming traffic. Thank God none is there.

I am now one heaving, shaking, pulsating mass of hysteria. I don't have a clue how I am moving this car forward, but somehow I manage to make it up to a traffic light. I see a police car up ahead of me waiting for the light to turn green. I slam on my brakes, jump out and rush up to the car.

I am watching myself banging on his window and I can hear something coming out of my mouth. Not words, though. What in the world is that noise? I'm not sure. My system starts to shut down and I find myself beginning to check out. All protective mechanisms are turning off. Let's put her to sleep now. Go to sleep. Let go.

And sleep I did—for what seemed like days. It was quite a while before I was in a position to step back and examine what had transpired in my life—to try to understand all the complex ramifications and implications. When I finally was, I began to make some amazing discoveries, many of which I have shared with you in this book.

And please know this. My observations stem from my subjective experiences. I am on a learning journey through this lifetime and, accordingly, view each experience as an opportunity to grow, expand and move forward. I will never have all the answers, but I am committed to becoming more aware of what is going on around me—to becoming more of a conscious student.

It all boils down to this. We all have a never ending source for power available to us at all times. How do we get it? It is ours for the asking, ours for the trusting. It lives *within* us, it expresses *as* us, and it can serve all of creation *through* us.

And how do we use it? We can use it consciously and wisely to evolve ourselves forward or we can misuse it and cause ourselves to implode and self-destruct. We have that choice.

And finally, we share it by giving freely and serving compassionately, enriching ourselves and others in the process.

All of these things are up to you and me. They are *all* a matter of choice. Of course they would be. Remember the definition of power I proposed earlier? Power is the ability to choose. This is true power.

And you've always had that power. It can never, ever be taken away from you. You are free to create the reality you choose. You are the *embodiment* of true power.

Bibliography

Bargh, J. A., Chen, M., Burrows. L. "Automaticity of Social Behavior: Direct effects of trait construct and stereotype priming on action." *Journal of Personality and Social Psychology.* 1996. pp. 71, 230-244.

Barker, Joel Arthur. *Paradigms: The Business of Discovering the Future.* New York: HarperCollins, 1992.

Borysenko, Joan. *Minding the Body, Mending the Mind.* New York: Bantam Books, 1987.

Branden, Nathaniel. *The Six Pillars of Self-Esteem.* New York: Bantam Books, 1994.

Csikszentmihalyi, Mihalyi. *Flow.* New York: Harper & Row, 1990.

Cousins, Norman. *Anatomy of an Illness.* New York: Bantam Books, 1979.

Covey, Stephen R. *The 7 Habits of Highly Effective People.* Provo, Utah: Franklin Covey Co., 1989, 1997. (Audiotapes)

_____, *Principle-Centered Leadership.* Provo, Utah: Franklin Covey Co., 1992, 1994. (Audiotapes)

Gallwey, W. Timothy. *The Inner Game of Tennis.* New York: Bantam Books, 1974.

Goleman, Daniel. *Emotional Intelligence.* New York: Bantam Books, 1995.

Hall, Doug. *Jump Start Your Brain.* New York: Warner Books, 1995.

His Holiness the Dalai Lama and Howard C. Cutler, M.D. *The Art of Happiness.* New York, Penguin Putnam, Inc. 1998.

Kehoe, John. *Mind Power.* Zoetic Inc.: Vancouver, 1997.

Keys, Ken. *Handbook to High Consciousness.* Marina Del Rey, Calif.: Living Love Pubications, 1980.

Larsen, Linda. *12 Secrets to High Self Esteem.* SkillPath Publishing Audio: 1999. (Audiotapes)

McGraw, Phillip C. *Life Strategies.* New York: Hyperion, 1999.

Mehrabian, Albert. *Silent Messages: Implicit Communication of Emotions and Attitudes.* Belmont, Calif.: Wadsworth Publishing, 1981.

Murphy, Joseph. *The Power of Your Subconscious Mind.* New York: Bantam Books, 1963, 1982.

Nelson, Bob. *1001 Ways to Energize Employees.* New York: Workman Publishing, 1997.

Nhat Hanh, Thich. *The Miracle of Mindfulness.* Boston: Beacon Press. 1975, 1976.

Peters, Tom. *Thriving on Chaos.* NewYork: HarperCollins, 1987.

Robbins, Anthony. *Awaken the Giant Within.* New York: Fireside Simon & Shuster, Inc., 1991.

Senge, Peter. *The Fifth Discipline.* New York: Currency Doubleday, 1990.

Sheldrake, Rupert. *Dogs That Know When Their Owners Are Coming Home and Other Unexplained Powers of Animals,* Crown, 1999.

Thompson, Charles "Chic." *What a Great Idea.* New York: HarperCollins, 1992.

Tracy, Brian. *The Psychology of Achievement.* Chicago: Nightingale Conant Audio.

Vanzant, Iyanla. *One Day My Soul Just Opened Up.* New York: Fireside Simon & Schuster, Inc., 1998.

Walsch, Neale Donald. *Conversations with God.* New York: G.P. Putnam's Sons, 1996.

Zukav, Gary. *Seat of the Soul.* New York: Fireside, 1989.

Index

A

acceptance, 97
action, 36, 68, 106
action ideas, 37–38, 58–60, 67–68, 80–81, 101
adventure, 41–42
advice, 86
Anatomy of an Illness, The, 112
anger
   controlling, 103–4
   past, 85
appreciation, 87
Aristotle, 103
art of mindfulness, 59
assumptions, 25–26
attitude, 26, 42–43, 46, 90–91, 108–9
audio tapes, 116, 118, 120
automaticity of being, 112
autopilot, 23, 24
   getting off, 25–26

B

Baez, Joan, 106
Bargh, John A., 112
Barton, Bruce, 58
behaviors, 20, 25
   and emotions, 106–8
   and results, 106–8
   self-defeating, 24, 26, 34–35, 110

beliefs, 25–26
brainstorming sessions, 77, 80
Brothers, Dr. Joyce, 110
burnout, 122–23
Burns, George, 77

C

career, 120
cause and effect, 63
challenges, 71–72
choices, 27, 40–41, 129
Chrysler, Walter, 43
clear communication, 99–101
comfort zone, 24, 119
communication, 93–101
   action ideas, 101
   body language, 93–96
   clear, 99–101
   facial expressions, 94–96
   and feelings, 99–100
   listening skills, 98
   listening to others, 97–99, 101
   and responses, 94–97, 101
   silent, 93
   verbal, 93–94
   visual, 93–97
   vocal, 93–94
competent, 24, 115
compromising needs, 34–35
confidence, 58, 60
connecting with people, 36
conscious mind, 53–55, 111
control, gaining, 14, 16
controlling destiny, 36
Conversations with God, 49
Cousins, Dr. Norman, 112
Covey, Dr. Stephen R., 39, 116
creativity
   and laughter, 78–79

loss of, 77–78
crediting others, 85
Csikszentmihalyi, Mihaly, 57

D

depression, 15
despair, 15
discipline, 26
Disney, Walt, 29
Dogs That Know When When Their Owners are Coming Home and Other Unexplained Powers of Animals, 65
drawing people, 96–97
Dryden, John, 21

E

Edison, Thomas, 43,44
education, 115–23. *See also* learning
  audio tapes, 116, 118, 120
  books, 120
  obtaining, 120
  planning, 120
  power of, 115, 116
  reading, 116
  reinforcing, 118
  retaining, 118
  seminars, 120
effective leaders, 71
effectiveness, 123
Einstein, Albert, 61, 71, 81, 109
emotions
  focus, 106
  impacting behavior, 106–8
  managing, 103, 105, 106
  mastering, 103–14
  result from thoughts, 105, 108
  and success cycle, 106
Emerson, Ralph Waldo, 47
energy
  conservation of, 63–64

electromagnetic, 65
positive, 43, 69
enthusiasm, 43–44
envisioning goals, 29–34. *See also* vision
envisioning the future, 35–36
excuses, 26–27

F

facial expressions, 93–97
Faster: The Acceleration of Just About Everything, 117
fear, overcoming, 121, 122
feedback, 25
Feel the Fear and Do It Anyway, 121
finances, 36, 119, 120, 121
flow, 56–58
focus, 57–58, 60, 106, 109, 113

G

getting out of the way, 51–58
getting results, 68, 69
giving freely, 85–86, 109–10
giving up, 71
Gleick, 117
God, 57, 56, 57, 60
gratitude, 109
grievances, past, 85

H

habits, 19–21, 25, 26–27
habitual patterns, 23, 24, 74–75
health, improving, 36, 120, 123
held captive, 13–15, 57, 61–62, 99, 125–28
helping others, 91
holding box, 33
honesty, 101
hours available, 117–18
humor, 78–79, 80–81
hurt, past, 85

I

idea generation, 71–81

finding, 71–81
and laughter, 78–79, 80–81
positive, 88–90
possible solutions, 75–77
and questions, 72–75
impressions on others, 63–64
intentions, 69
internal dialogue, 87–88, 110, 113
interpretations, 39–40, 41–42, 45, 47–50
interrelationships, 63
intimidation, 96
Isen, Alice, 78

J

James, William, 51
Jeffers, Dr. Susan, 121
Journal of Personality and Social Psychology, 78
Jung, Carl, 39

K

Kaizen, 115
Killer Phrases, 79–81
KZ strategy, 84–88

L

laughter, 78–79, 80–81
learning
  audio tapes, 116, 118, 120
  books, 116, 120
  ease of, 116, 118
  journey, 128
  lifelong, 115–23
  obtaining, 120
  reinforcing, 118
  retaining, 118
  seminars, 120
life, mastering, 36
Life Mastery, 51, 120
Life Strategies, 97
lifelong learning, 115–23. *See also* learning

listening skills, 98
listening well, 97–99, 101
loyalty, 101

M

managing emotions, 103, 105, 106
mantra, 60, 113–14
mastering emotions, 103–14
mastery, 57–58
material things, 36
McGraw, Dr. Phillip C., 97
Mehrabian, Dr. Albert, 94
meditation, 59–60
mental aspects of life, 123
mind
    conscious mind, 53–55, 111
    subconscious mind, 53–55, 111
mind, body, and spirit, 68
mindfulness, art of, 59
Mindshift, 115
misery, overcoming, 31–32, 34–36
morale, boosting, 91
motivating people, 91. *See also* stories that motivate

N

negative thoughts, 79–81, 110
negative words, 79, 110–12
Nietzche, Frederick, 37
Nightingale, Earl, 116

O

objective look at self, 25–27, 34–35, 94, 110
opinions, 86

P

people around you, 25, 36, 83–84, 91, 93, 96–98, 108–9
persuasion, 42–43
Peters, Tom, 73
phrases, negative, 79–81
physical aspects of life, 123

physiology, 106–7
pleasure/pain principle, 32–33
positive attitude, 42–43, 46, 90–91, 108–9
positive energy, 43, 69
power, 14, 15, 21, 57, 123
    ability to choose, 50
    accessing, 128
    of animals, 65
    to create, 123
    of education, 115, 116
    habits, 21–22
    illusion of, 16
    never-ending source, 128–29
    of persuasion, 42–43
    positive, 16, 42–43, 46, 50, 64
    reconnecting with, 25–26
    sharing, 128
    strategies for, 37–38, 84–88
    temporary feeling of, 96
    true, 16, 18
    using, 128
    within self, 128
powerful people, 29–30, 95–96
powerful thinking, 65–67
powerful words, 110–12
practicing your craft, 58–60
principles, 47
Pritchett, Price, 115
problems, eliminating, 71–72

Q

questions
    as idea-generators, 72–75
    and negative responses, 88
    positive, 88–90
    possible solutions, 75–77

R

rapport, establishing, 97, 98, 99

reading, benefits of, 116
reaffirm new thoughts, 67
reconnecting to true power, 25–26
relationships, 36, 83–91, 101, 120
resentment, 85
response to events, 39, 41–42
results, 68, 69
   from behavior, 106–8
   successful, 123
   from thoughts, 105, 108
retaining information, 118
right events, 87, 90–91
right words, 110–12
risks, taking, 119
roadmap, 123
Robbins, Anthony, 51, 120

S

Satir, Virginia, 93
secret of success, 43
self, care of, 36, 68, 120, 122–23
self-defeating behaviors, 25–26, 34–35, 110
   strategies to overcome, 24
self-forgetfulness, 58
self-observation, 25, 27, 34–35, 94, 110
seminars, 120
Senge, Peter, 26
Seven Habits of Highly Effective People, The, 39, 123
Shakespeare, William, 56
sharing freely, 85–86, 109–10
Sheldrake, Rupert, 65
silent communication, 93
SkillPath Seminars, 122
Smith, Fred, 116
social aspects of life, 123
social self, 122–23
solutions, providing, 71–81
   action ideas, 80–81
   finding, 71–80

idea generation, 75–80
spiritual aspects of life, 123
spiritual self, 122–23
stories that motivate, 39, 41–42, 44–46, 47–48, 49–50
strategies for power, 84–88
   action ideas, 37–38
strategies for success, 17–18
subconscious mind, 53–55, 111
success cycle, 106–8
success, secret of, 43
success, strategies for, 17–18
survivor, 14
systems thinking, 61, 62

T

taking care of self, 36, 68, 120, 122–23
taking risks, 119
talking to ourselves, 87–88, 110, 113
thank-you notes, 87
The Fifth Discipline, 26
Thompson, Charles "Chic," 79
Thoreau, Henry David, 56
thoughts as matter, 64–65
thoughts as power, 65–67, 105, 108
   action ideas, 67–68
time, wasted, 116, 117
   hours available, 117–18
   Tomlin, Lily, 29
Tracy, Brian, 83, 116
true power, 16, 18, 25–26, 129. *See also* power
Truman, Harry, 116
trust, 51–52, 53, 60, 94
truth, 25
Twain, Mark, 110, 111

U

unconditional love, 85–86

V

verbal communication, 93–94

vision, 29–36
  action ideas, 37–38
  creating, 30, 33–34, 36–37, 64–65, 122
visual communication, 93–97
vocal communication, 93–94

W

Wagner, Jane, 29
Walsch, Neale Donald, 49
What a Great Idea, 79
wisdom, 56–57
  accessing, 58–60
workshops, 120

Z

Ziglar, Zig, 91
Zukov, Gary, 19, 69

About the Author

Linda Larsen is an award-winning, international keynote speaker and best-selling author who is passionately committed to helping people bring the very best version of themselves to life every single day. Her belief is that how we show up in the world, the attitudes we bring with us and the perspectives we hold have a direct impact on the quality of our lives. The health of our relationships, how good we are at solving problems and coming up with new ideas, the level of the customer service we provide, and even how happy and healthy we are - all trace back to who we are, what we believe, and the choices we make moment-to-moment. Her mission is to share ideas and strategies that will help people live their absolute best life ever.

With a bachelor's degree in social work, a master's degree in fine arts and extensive training in personal development, Linda also holds a CSP (Certified Speaking Professional), the highest earned designation in the speaking industry. Additionally she worked as a trial consultant for over 10 years, helping attorneys communicate more persuasively and effectively in the high stakes, high stress environment of the courtroom. Linda was also a professional actor for over 20 years on stage, films & television with such notables as the late Sid Caesar, Beau Bridges and Ed Harris.

To have Linda contribute to the success of your next conference, visit her website at www.lindalarsen.com. There you can see which of her topics would be best for your goup and watch her in action in her online videos. You can also contact her at 941-927-4700.